THE
AUTISM
PROPHECIES

How an Evolution of Healers and Intuitives
Is Influencing Our Spiritual Future

WILLIAM STILLMAN

A division of The Career Press, Inc.
Franklin Lakes, NJ

THE AUTISM PROPHECIES
EDITED BY GINA HOOGERHYDE
TYPESET BY DIANA GHAZZAWI
Cover design by The Book Designers
Printed in the U.S.A. by Courier

To order this title, please call toll-free 1-800-CAREER-1 (NJ and Canada: 201-848-0310) to order using VISA or MasterCard, or for further information on books from Career Press.

The Career Press, Inc., 3 Tice Road, PO Box 687,
Franklin Lakes, NJ 07417
www.careerpress.com
www.newpagebooks.com

Library of Congress Cataloging-in-Publication Data

Stillman, William, 1963-
    The autism prophecies : how an evolution of healers and intuitives is influencing our spiritual future / by William Stillman.
        p. cm.
    Includes index.
    ISBN 978-1-60163-116-9 (pbk.) – ISBN 978-1-60163-734-5 (e book) 1. Autism. 2. Spirituality. I. Title.
    RC553.A88.S836 2010
    616.85'882--dc22
                                                                                            2009051732

For Michael Hricko, Michael Logan, and Wally Wojtowicz, Jr., with all my love.

Acknowledgments

Thank you, Lord, for all the gifts and blessings and privileges that have been bestowed upon me in this lifetime. I am doing my best to honor my exceptional good fortune by being a bridge for others, with grace and humility.

Gratitude is due to my longtime literary agent, June Clark, for her personal and professional interest in me and all that I have to offer.

Appreciations go to the following individuals for illuminating the truth by sharing their experiences with me: John Quincy Adams, Ann Marie Akash, Gary Averill, Tara Bangham, Tricia Baum, Laurence Becker, L.J. Benzi, Ursula and Singen Bowler, Larry Brody, Rhonda and Jordan Brunett, William Carpenter, Renee Chastain, Carol Creel, Traci Cornette, Donna and Christopher Cully, Anne-Laure Davin, Ryland Davis, Nick Dubin, Erica Eames, Jeannie Lloyd Ginther, Matthew Gromis, Annette Harkness, Mary Ann Harrington, Richele Hemesath, Julia Howerin, Michael Hricko, Pamela Kline, Izzy and Deb Kranzel, Petra Kroger, Richie Leitner, Lucy Lewis, Michael Logan, George Machado, Dawn Melton, Michelle Miller, Michael Nagula, Reverend Ziek Paterniti, Roia Raefian, Mark Reeves, Jamie Shallenberger, Leesa Shusta, Kathryn Stonehouse, Melissa Stupak, Birgit and Fred Werth, James Wilson, Linda Yale, Teo Zagar, and Maria Zalucki.

Special thanks to Wally and Gay Wojtowicz, and Wally Wojtowicz, Jr., for ensuring that Wally's sage perspectives are documented and reproduced in this volume in their entirety.

Annette Becklund, William Gaventa, Lisa Martinelli, Dr. Mary Riposo, and Sandra Sedgbeer (*Children of the New Earth* online magazine) were gracious enough to circulate my survey to interested parties, and I am grateful to them for their interest and support.

Contents

Introduction ✳ 11

Part One: Healers

Chapter 1: The Mechanics of Miracles ✳ 23

Chapter 2: The Art of Healing ✳ 29

Part Two: Mysterious Ways

Chapter 3: Impossible Gifts ✳ 51

Chapter 4: Knowledge Is Power ✳ 77

Chapter 5: Spiritual Warfare ✳ 87

Part Three: Future Forecasts

Chapter 6: A Remarkable Revelation ✳ 127

Chapter 7: Casting the Net ✳ 135

Chapter 8: Wally's Wisdom ✳ 163

Chapter 9: Conclusions ✳ 193

Index ✳ 201

About the Author ✳ 205

Introduction

One day my young friend, Fred, was lying on his bed making the kind of repetitious vocalizing that has become accepted as a stereotypical mannerism of so many persons diagnosed with autism. "*Au...au... au...*" he warbled with perseveration. But because Fred's mother Birgit presumed his intelligence, she knew better than to believe that the vocalizations were merely gibberish. Instead, she asked him to *type* what it was he was attempting so diligently to articulate. He wrote, "Autism," to which Birgit replied, "What about it?" Fred answered, "Autism is not a disease. God made us this way." Birgit pressed him, "What about vaccinations and environmental toxins? What role do they play?" Fred's answer conveyed comprehension light-years beyond his youthful chronology, "God gave us these sensitivities to show how nature is in distress. He wants us people to slow down. We are like lighthouses. Autism is telling my world that it is not paying attention to the signs."

Not paying attention to the signs is a concept I've espoused in two prior books, *Autism and the God Connection* and *The Soul of Autism,* which reveal a viable association between some individuals with autism and the aptitude for acute spiritual sensitivity. Wouldn't it be the most delicious of ironies, I speculate, if those persons our society deems most severely impaired are actually among the keepers of keen insight and aesthetic awareness. And yet according this enlightened reverence to

11

people with autism—or anyone with a perceived disability—is far from the norm for an era in which I am routinely apprised of horror stories that speak of ignorance and intolerance against those very persons. (For recently reported citations of abuse, please see *www.neurodiversity.com/ abuse.html* or the Children Injured by Restraints and Aversives Website at *http://users.1st.net/cibra/index.htm.*)

Hannah Arendt, in her book, *The Origins of Totalitarianism*, suggests that torture—mistreatment and humiliation enacted from a self-righteous perpetrator to a victim condemned—is not only the linchpin of total domination, but results in "the murder of the moral person." A component of the 2009 Obama administration's agenda was the promise to restore civility by renouncing "enhanced interrogation" techniques employed under the previous presidential administration. Obama's position was not only one of nobility, it was egregiously overdue.

Yet the mistreatment and humiliation—including the unholy denouement of the moral person—that Obama sought to minimize, if not eradicate, is very much alive and well, and occurring in this precise moment. Whereas such unconscionable insults against prisoner detainees and other minorities are an embarrassing smear on our country's conduct (and would be enforceable for felony prosecution under any other circumstances), similar—if not identical—tactics are routinely applied to manage, control, and maintain our citizens with autism. I am aware of such school students being slapped, punched, pinched, bitten, strapped to chairs, and locked in closets, or students who have had their mouths muted by silvery duct-tape. Oftentimes the abuse perpetrated is defended, condoned, or concealed. An inequitable dichotomy is apparent when we seek to reconcile past transgressions in the name of grace and humanitarianism, *but* we persist in sanctioning parallel affronts that are both disgraceful and dehumanizing in the name of *treatment.*

Instead certain media celebrities—"warrior mothers"—have emerged as spokespersons to proffer the resolve that led to the "recovery" of their children from autism. Most are very young parents of very young children, and whether those children will undoubtedly retain the autistic aspect of their personalities well into adulthood, it simply remains to be seen, in my opinion. I fully support respectful, reciprocal approaches to aid any individual with autism to tame and refine their experience in order to better appreciate their uniqueness. However, this all too often gets bastardized into a cure-at-any-cost mentality that fuels a culture of fear about autism which, in turn, feeds a multi-billion dollar industry of therapies, services, facilities, and methodologies. The darkest edge of that mix includes physical and mechanical-device restraints, and sedating anti-psychotic medication. The endeavor for *normalcy* permeates and persists in a society that idolizes perfection.

As I predicted in my 2008 book, *The Soul of Autism*, a prenatal test for autism, in the manner of detecting (and selecting to abort) fetuses with Down syndrome, is imminent. *The* (London) *Sunday Times* for January 18, 2009, in a piece by India Knight titled, "Soon We'll be on an Ugly Quest for Perfect Embryos," reports that the Autism Research Centre at Cambridge University found that "babies exposed to high levels of testosterone in the womb had a higher risk of developing autistic traits." High levels of testosterone were previously shown to be associated with "less eye contact by a child's first birthday, slower language development by their second birthday, more peer difficulties by their fourth birthday, and more difficulties with empathy by their sixth birthday." The conclusion being that, to paraphrase, autism is an acute manifestation of the male brain. (Males are four times more likely to have autism than females.) Director of the Autism Research Centre, Professor Simon Baron-Cohen, suggests that if ever a test to prevent autism indeed came to fruition (the implication being the option for termination of pregnancy), the potential to eradicate extraordinary talent would be considerable. "What else would be lost?" he asked. "Would we also reduce the number of future great mathematicians, for example?"

The quest for designer embryos and perfect babies calls into question innumerable ethical conflicts about honor, responsibility, and faith. As India Knight writes, "When it comes to a disease such as cancer, the agonies (in the instance of a pre-natal screening) the child's mother must have gone through seem worthwhile: you die of cancer. Nobody dies of autism." Not only doesn't anyone die of autism, in this author's opinion, autism fulfills an intention, and serves a real and viable purpose.

My young friend Michael, a contributor to both of my prior autism-and-spirituality books, calls us to task with regard to the ever-widening gap that creates an us-and-them paradigm in perceptions.

Division is a slippery slope; once me as severely disabled, why not you as differently-abled. What becomes the variation and measure? How much is too much difference? Societal norms dictate the measures used. Hitler created his own societal norm and the masses followed. The "cure-bie" mentality is not limited to autism. It is potentially aimed at each of us. Let us cure the world of "autists" or gays or blacks or whites for that matter, whoever is the odd man out at the time.

You do it now. Not with a pill or remedy, but with an attitude of superiority. Attitude is all it takes to destroy a soul. You can kill something just as easily this way as the other. How many have already been robbed of their personhood through therapies designed to teach normalcy. It is genocide already. For me to have to teach diversity appreciation places the victim in the position of responsibility. I am not sure I like that. It is the responsibility of the non-victims to speak.

Despite his tender years, Michael's concerns for a slippery slope of division hark to a period of separation between those differently-abled and able, which has its beginnings decades before he was ever born—a separation whose stronghold indelibly colors parental expectations to this day.

Our Egregious Past

I began my human services career in 1987 at a time when the word *autism* was practically unheard of. I worked in community residences with adults who, in hindsight, were clearly autistic, but were not clinically diagnosed as such; instead they were labeled with moderate, severe, or profound mental retardation. A few decades prior, those same individuals might've also been diagnosed schizophrenic. All the people to whom I provided care previously lived in institutions—self-contained state centers to which anyone considered defective (including children with epilepsy and cerebral palsy) was sent to live, to be taught or trained and raised by staff purportedly qualified to do so.

Today, new parents of very young children with autism may be unable to fathom the enormity and efficiency of state-run institutions, or that, without public school options, it was standard procedure for countless families to all but disown their children in favor of this attractive and placating opportunity. (In many instances parents were deliberately discouraged from having contact with their children for the ease of transition.) It was part and parcel of a eugenics movement—the reduction of certain people and traits—designed to segregate undesirables from mainstream society. For example, a pictorial prospectus from the now-notorious Pennhurst State School in Spring City, Pennsylvania, dated 1954, gives an overview of its idyllic facilities. Among its opulent offerings:

✳ An on-site hospital and school (including vocational training).

✳ Dining halls, kitchens, and butcher shop.

✳ A reservoir, disposal plant, power plant, and water tower.

✳ An automotive fleet, storeroom, and laundry.

✳ A fully-equipped farm with cattle, pigs, hens, gardens, and orchards.

✳ Accommodations to serve upward of 3,500 individuals.

Institutional settings were also ripe for physical, mental, and sexual abuse perpetrated against its patients, or "inmates," as they were known. Public exposure of such offenses at Pennhurst led to the first lawsuit of its kind, asserting the rights of people with developmental disabilities to education and life in their respective communities; this 1977 ruling eventually led to the establishment of the Americans with Disabilities Act.

In those beginning days of my employment, I worked alongside people who had been warehoused at Pennhurst and other facilities, and somehow survived the murder of the moral person. This was the era when autism was considered extremely rare, said to affect 1 in 10,000 children. More than 20 years later, there are data-collection procedures in place to more accurately reflect the rate of autism and other so-called childhood anomalies.

A RISING EVOLUTION

Popular media may mislead us in the belief that autism is a phenomenon isolated to the United States. It's not. It is transpiring worldwide. There are approximately 1.5 million people with autism here, but those numbers are also comparable with China's estimates. Our statistics indicate 1 in 110 children have autism, but in Ireland it's also 1 in 110, and in Great Britain it's variously believed to affect either 1 in 100 or 1 in 58 children depending upon the reference. Indeed, a July 10, 2008 report from the Vaccine Autoimmune Project suggests the prevalence of autism in the U.S. is underestimated, and 1 in 67 children affected would be a more realistic reflection of the true numbers. Autism shows no signs of abating despite research, studies, awareness, and fund-raising. And at this rate, concurrent with research efforts, it's high time we alter our focus not just for what causes autism, but what autism *causes*.

In response to my books, I have the routine pleasure of hearing from parents who have undergone a positive personal transformation with autism as the catalyst. (It amuses me to tell you that more than a few have had my texts fall from a shelf at their feet in bookstores and libraries.) They are writing to affirm my contentions, and to explain how raising a child with autism has compelled them to slow down, to evaluate what's important, and to aspire a life that is authentic instead of cluttered with the false idols of our present society: wealth, physical beauty, material possessions, and self-gratification. In many cases, families have been drawn to religion or spirituality (even where such was previously void) by their inherently gentle and exquisitely sensitive son or daughter. Richele is one such parent, mom to son Tanner. Tanner is painfully sensitive, "surpassing any earthly explanation" according to Richele. She explains:

> In the autumn of Tanner's first-grade year, I recall watching my son as he and his classmates were pulling the annuals from the garden in front of their school, which they had planted the previous spring. Tanner's favorite flowers are snapdragons. As the teacher began pulling the snapdragons from the earth, my son fell to his knees and cried. When his teacher asked him what was wrong, he replied, "I feel so sad for the snapdragons. They have given us great beauty. They

don't deserve to die." Tanner sat on my lap and cried for a very long time. That same autumn, as Tanner and I were enjoying a stroll on a particularly crisp and radiant autumn day, Tanner became upset when I stepped on some gorgeous red and orange leaves which had fallen from a maple tree. He said, "We must have respect for all living things. Please don't step on the leaves." And so I didn't.

Regrettably, the intensity of Tanner's sensitivity predisposed him to be the object of insensitive harassment by his peers. Instead of heeding the advice from educators and school administrators that Tanner needed to "toughen up" and "grow a thicker skin," Richele listened to her mother's heart when, in the third grade, Tanner considered suicide. "I recall him saying throughout that enormously difficult time that he felt as though his soul had left his body," she related. Faced with the only alternative, Richele and her husband made the decision to withdraw Tanner from his school district and homeschool him. Thankfully, Tanner's traumatic experiences did not quiet his astute and compassionate insights, and Richele shares one of Tanner's symbolic similes, the kind to which I've grown accustomed in communicating with those who have autism.

I recall one ordinary evening when Tanner was 7, and my husband and I and Tanner's sister were going about our usual routine. Tanner was drawing in our living room when, out of the blue, he said, "Mom, get some paper and a writing utensil! You might want to write these down. I'm sharing them with you because I think they're worth sharing."

Tanner: "We are who we are and that is the way life should be. Do you know what this means, mom?"

Me: "I'm not sure...why don't you explain it to me?"

Tanner: "It means you should be who you are, not try to be someone else just to get friends. You'll get friends for being who you are sooner or later. The wise frog will be still while waiting for the fly. The wise frog does not seek out the fly."

Again, Tanner asked me if I knew what this meant and I asked him to explain it.

Tanner: "It means that with patience come rewards."

We are who we are, and that is the way life should be, certainly
runs counter to the preceding history lesson. Abuse and mistreatment
persists because of fear. But the culture of fear we purvey is not a fear
of our differences between us and them, it is a fear of our collective
similarities—a discomfort for confronting the truth about our own idio-
syncrasies. This is precisely why the brightly beaming man with Down
syndrome who greets shoppers at Wal-Mart is completely ignored, or
the person struggling to articulate spoken language gets tuned out and
disregarded.

Curiously, the original intent of the aforementioned eugenics movement, the motto of which was, "eugenics is the self-direction of human
evolution," is actually transpiring in reverse. Unlike Hitler's Nazi
Germany and his eugenic vision of engineering a race of supermen—and
despite our disgraceful history of sterilization, segregation, and ostraciz-
ing of those deemed different—autism is slowly but surely contributing momentum to a new evolution that is supplanting anyone's ideal of
genetic or hereditary perfection. Does this foretell of the rewards reaped
from the patience Tanner advises us to hold?

Thank goodness human beings have burgeoned beyond the capacity of Neanderthals, the *homo sapiens* subspecies that originated up to
600,000 years ago, and from which modern man, in part, evolved. That
evolutionary process took thousands of years, but with God all things
are possible and, if a new evolution is occurring right before our eyes,
what's to suggest it would have to play out in an identical time frame?
Using the 1 in 110 children statistic, someone (probably someone with
autism) crunched the numbers and projected the date of 2035 when
the majority of the population has the potential to be autistic! Given
the personal, parental, and cultural impact autism is imposing on an
unforgiving world I wouldn't be at all surprised if, within the next five
to 10 years, the statistics of autism's incidence in children doesn't leap
to 1 in 10. (In the fall of 2009, reporter David Kirby blogged that the
National Survey of Children's Health, which is supported by the Health
Resources and Services Administration of the U.S. Department of Health
and Human Services, released data from a 2007 telephone survey of
parents of nearly 82,000 U.S. children, which concluded that the odds

of a parent being told that their child has autism are now 1 in 63. Kirby advises, "If it is a boy, the chances climb to a science fiction-like level of *1 in 38, or 2.6 percent of all male children in America*.")

THE BEACON THAT BECKONS

This position is not intended as an alarmist's prediction of a sweeping plague or vengeful punishment, but as an *opportunity* for wisdom and knowledge beyond the wars and the hardships and the appalling misconduct that has become an acceptable way of life for so many. If we can avail ourselves to some (or all) of this stance, we may be better able to shift away from prejudice and hate, and move ever-closer toward an era of enlightenment. It is imminent.

Even as I was engrossed in compiling *Autism and the God Connection*, the first book to embrace these themes, I recognized the necessity of exercising caution by deliberately revealing the truth of my experiences and encounters in *increments*. I had long envisioned a trilogy of books that would encompass this information, and the volume you now hold succeeds the second book, *The Soul of Autism*, in unveiling more of what remains—extraordinary examples of the spiritual possibilities God holds for *us all*, but which are, perhaps, most readily accessible to those who have deceiving physical exteriors. The term *prophecies*, of this book's title, pertains not only to the projections of the last several chapters, it incorporates many other aspects of autism that, if properly cultivated, could have proactive ramifications for us all. In addition to forecasts for humanity's collective future, capabilities counted as *natural* not *supernatural* include the capacity for healing, discerning positive spiritual interactions, and understanding the universe of thought. Herein I also illuminate a spiritual power struggle I've witnessed emerging with increasing fervor—important information for families to distinguish their child's legitimate plight from clinical criteria.

Our moral code has become nearly baseless, and our society requires a return to civility and grace. In increasing numbers, humankind is clearing aside disillusionment, and disassociating from the toxic decay of that which is not authentic. It shows in a growing intolerance for corporate corruption, political deception, economic erosion, the violence of pornography, and religious scandal. (For example, the 2008

U.S. Religious Landscape Survey, conducted on 35,566 adults, indicates spiritual unbelief and unconcern with formal religious distinctions is on the rise.) Our present economic recession is unlike anything seen by the United States since the 1930s, and yet it is compelling people to be frugal, innovative, and resourceful—necessary attributes for a renaissance of altruistic priorities.

In its silent manner, autism contributes its own paradoxical query to the fray: is its very prevalence the result of myriad medicinal, environmental, and genetic toxins, or is its existence the *antidote* for all that is toxic in the world? If we can embrace the latter position, then Fred's lighthouse for autism becomes an apt metaphor—the beacon that beckons us, one and all, as we continue our journey of hope toward the attainment of mutual understanding, compassion, and respect.

PART ONE
HEALERS

Chapter 1

The Mechanics of Miracles

"We are the future of a kinder world."
—Mark Reeves, consultant and
person with autism

When we think of modern-day healers, the first thing that may come to mind is medical practitioners—skilled surgeons and seasoned physicians who ameliorate or rectify the physical ailments of others. When we think of *miraculous* healers, we may conjure thoughts of old-world saints, or even Jesus Christ, who performed spontaneous acts of recovery in those afflicted. Yet saints weren't always saints; saints were citizens—*ordinary* citizens who heeded a calling, and who applied the best of what they had to offer in their station as inspired human beings.

In my book, *Autism and the God Connection*, I write of my first encounter with an apparent act of healing, an instance that took time to appreciate because I didn't recognize it in the moment it occurred. While making a home visit, Kevin, a young, non-speaking boy with autism, quickly and suddenly struck out and "karate-chopped" a professional colleague on the shoulder. Everyone present instantly leaped to the assumption that this incident was a stereotypical act of physical aggression, believed to commonly coincide in many boys with autism, and Kevin was reprimanded for his behavior. But afterward, on our return trip, my colleague confided that he had, for the past couple days, been grappling with a painful knot in his shoulder that restricted his movement. That knotted muscle was now relieved—the exact same spot upon which Kevin had leveled his strike with the deft precision of a surgeon. Fluke or fate?

This event piqued my curiosity and caused me to reflect on perceptions and misperceptions, and the untold aptitude of those who naturally dwell in silence for not being able to speak. I have advocated at great length throughout my career the principle for presuming the intelligence of those with autism who, in the physical, *appear to be* significantly impaired but, with proper communication methods, can demonstrate an authentic and fully capable personhood. (If this concept is novel to the reader, kindly direct your attention to any number of my written works for further detail.) I have conjectured that, if we always presume the competence of the person within, the non-verbal individual with autism exists in a perpetual state of meditation—always pondering, reflecting, considering, processing, and very carefully observing. If we believe the person to hold mental faculties every bit as intact as someone with, say, cerebral palsy, then their intrinsic state of solitude (alluding to the very definition of the word *autism*) becomes equable with—if not surpassing of—those who *intentionally* enter into a parallel state: the nun, the monk, the yogi, or the guru. Those whom we may hold in reverence for their spiritual regard pray or meditate to attain a heightened connection with our Source. This heightened connection may manifest with an enhanced sensitivity, compassion, or even gifted ability and a similar process undergone by those with autism would be bound to yield comparable fruit, as I've previously speculated and documented.

A Course in Miracles focuses on the healing of the mind over the illusion of our physical selves. This resonates when we consider an aforementioned dichotomy of consciousness for many individuals with autism: the cerebral is whole and intact, but the physical is usually not of good service. If we can accept that those with autism, who are inherently gentle and exquisitely sensitive, buzz and vibrate at a higher frequency—as it relates to all the senses—then the challenge to literally integrate with the physical becomes quite the struggle. (In classic autism there is an untarnished purity of senses, much the same as members of the animal kingdom perceive the world without societal filters. See Temple Grandin's *Animals in Translation* for further detail.) This reflects in real time via acute, painful, and overwhelming sensory sensitivities (succumbing to an overload of external stimuli), as well as limited mobility (arms, legs, and trunk are desynchronized), and speech delays. Quite simply, the unusual pairing of aesthetics and high-thought within a body that feels like cement makes for strange bedfellows. But such is the plight of countless people with autism who struggle not only with this complex assimilation process, but also with the gross misunderstanding and imposed behavioral conditioning deemed as commensurate with their so-called disability.

How, then, do we get from this prospect (contrasts between gifted-yet-maligned persons with autism and persons of traditional spiritual elevation) to the concept of healing capacity, as was apparently the case with young Kevin, when the empathy required for so altruistic an act *contradicts* the empathic void dictated by clinical definitions of autism? To begin, I wish to revisit a theory I introduced in my book, *The Soul of Autism*: harmonious patterns or *entrainment*. This alignment of heart and mind commonly happens to us *individually* in times of absorbing focus, such as when we are immersed in creating something or are deep in solitary thought (showering, jogging, gardening)—we are open to a stream of consciousness and inspiration impressed within us; it happens to us *collectively* when hearts and minds align between one another, such as when we spontaneously share an experience with a loved one (thinking of someone and they text us in that moment, or chortling together at an inside joke).

It is entrainment that causes those moments when we are in the zone, so to speak, which manifests heightened creativity of thought and deed, or a heartfelt and personal connection with others. These moments resonate not only because of the connection, but because of the *emotion* associated with them. From these occasions comes unlimited possibilities for human potential in the way that people congregate for prayer vigils, for example; it is with the intention that the spiritual entrainment—the harmonious patterns—will compel a miraculous resolve through divine intervention. And while the resolve may not always come in the expected manner, the results from such procedures (such as a sudden remission of cancer) have been complicated in the extreme, and sensationalized as otherworldly. Instead, the human potential for unlimited possibilities is *normal* not *paranormal*—the birthright of humankind.

Championing Chad

I know from my experience as a consultant that I am only as good as my attunement with each individual with autism for whom I am consulting. I work intuitively—much differently from other professionals who require hours and hours of observation time, data collection, and assessments. I require only a matter of minutes in the presence of the person with autism to achieve a level of understanding necessary to advise his or her support team. It is for this reason that I purposefully enter into each consultation "cold"; that is, at the risk of undue influence I want to know absolutely *nothing* in advance about the individual except for their name and age. Such was the case when it was arranged for me to meet Chad, a 17-year-old young man with autism who was more than 6-feet tall, more than 200 pounds, and non-verbal. However, approaching Chad with a belief in his competence, I quietly introduced myself and thanked him for adjusting his schedule to meet with me. I also made a point of letting him know that I recognized his keen intelligence.

The more I spoke to Chad softly, gently, and with great compassion, the more he understood: I was not there to "treat" him; I was there to teach others how to correctly interpret him as an intelligent being, an intellectual peer precluded from demonstrating the truth of his personhood by a roadblock named autism. Chad wept in relief of this realization, and I pledged to honor my words as we embraced good-bye. What I later learned was that for the remainder of that day, Chad was happy and smiling. I was also informed that he had a reputation for being so very violent and out of control that everyone kept him at arm's length—and here I had been in a room alone with Chad, seated next to him, and with my arm around his shoulder as I counseled and consoled him!

The entrainment I experienced with Chad was a palpable alignment of hearts and minds in compassionate synchronization. I understood his difficulty integrating with a body that wasn't reliable for him, so I disregarded that aspect of his humanity and, instead, favored the intelligence dormant within him. More than a year later, when Chad and I reunited, he typed on a portable keyboard, "You read my mind not my body." (This is sound advice for anyone struggling to come to terms with autism.) Because of the entrainment we shared, my *relationship* with Chad was unique, and from this, there was enormous potential for growth.

KING OF LOVE

A relationship virtually identical was shared with me by Rob:

To help make ends meet, I took a second job working for an agency that specializes in the needs of autistic persons. That is how I met Ralph. He is 6-foot, 8-inches tall, about 250 pounds, and unable to speak. He stands out. Ralph is not able to direct the use of his hands or actions well. He has lots of neurological/behavioral/medical issues. He was diagnosed as severely retarded until his mother discovered, through a communication technique involving typing called Facilitated Communication (FC), that he was quite cognizant of his surroundings; perhaps more aware than anyone I have ever known.

I hope you will understand the confidential nature of this story when I tell you that Ralph and I communicate through a combination of telepathy and FC. I have always considered myself to be of a religious/scientific mind and as such I keep it as open as possible, constantly trying to root out bad information and falsehoods. When he first started FC with me I began to realize he was reading my mind. (Ralph said once, when I asked him how it was done, that "the message is the medium," meaning love.)

We carry on FC conversations. He reads my thoughts, questions, and comments, and responds on the FC keyboard. I do not know if others are aware of this. We never addressed it head-on for fear of losing our credibility with each other, I am afraid. And he is brilliant. I believe Ralph is able to read, interpret, and conclude a typed page of advanced thought at a glance. We read Dickens together (I turn the pages as he reads) at about eight seconds every two pages. His insights into the human condition are profound. He likes to watch C-SPAN and has no problem watching mundane broadcasts like the Congressional Budget Committee's presentations.

But far more amazing than his telepathy and genius is Ralph's connection to the Father. His love and spirituality are majestic and are unlike any I have ever known. I believe he is in constant communion with the Creator. To me, he calls himself "King Love." Frankly, he is my mentor, I am not his.

The type of bonding kinship I've enjoyed with Chad, and which Rob and Ralph have shared, is the essence of what drives the mechanics of miracles: unconditional love and the desire to be of service to others. Not rocket science, is it? Tara, mom to Tyler, her young son with Asperger's Syndrome, came to this realization herself.

Once we were at the beach. He was trying to teach me how to see auras. He put his feet and hands into the sand and told me this would help me to see the energies. He was very excited to tell me that my aura was very bright. I had a large ring of white and around that it was a beautiful red violet color. He could see the auras of all the birds. They were mostly purple and blue. He could see a red aura around a jogger and a brown aura around a bike rider. He observed that my boyfriend had a black, grayish aura, and he felt that he was upset about something but was holding it in. I confirmed that he was upset about our relationship because we were thinking about separating. I told Tyler that he didn't seem upset to me, but Tyler said he felt that is because he is holding the pain inside. He also told me that some special people have rainbow auras and that they're here to help the planet. It was an amazing lesson given by my very sensitive 10-year-old at the time.... At first I felt like this [diagnosis] was a bomb being dropped on me, but now I see it as a gift that just needs to be opened.

Not only did Tara come to appreciate her son's unconventional aptitude, but her relationship with him led to a form of healing in terms of acceptance. It is an attitude adopted by those parents who disarm, surrender the battle, and make peace with autism as an opportunity instead of an insult. But, I wondered, are there greater measures for healing on other levels beyond acceptance? I would soon come to know that Tyler's intuitive perception of others' energy was only the beginning.

Chapter 2

The Art of Healing

"The art of healing comes from nature, not from the physician.
Therefore the physician must start from nature,
with an open mind."
—Philipus Aureolus Paracelsus

When we think about the burgeoning field of alternative and integrative medicine, or energy work, the same principles that underlie entrainment also apply. Practitioners in this field attempt to manipulate individuals' energy fields by affecting the alignment of harmonious patterns, leading to a healing treatment. Biofield therapies are used to affect energy fields that purportedly surround and penetrate the human body. Examples include qi gong, Reiki, and Therapeutic Touch. Bioelectromagnetic-based therapies involve the unconventional use of electromagnetic fields, such as pulsed fields, magnetic fields, or alternating-current or direct-current fields.

Reiki has become an increasingly popular treatment modality, recognized and condoned by more than 60 hospitals in the United States. According to practitioner Bonnie Hassan's Website, "Allegheny General Hospital in Pittsburgh has a group of Reiki volunteers that offer Reiki treatments to patients after surgery to help their bodies process out the effects of anesthesia and to help the healing process. The Cleveland Clinic was recently awarded a $250,000 federal grant to study the effect of Reiki on prostate cancer patients." Reiki may also reduce the unwanted side effects of radiation and chemotherapy. Originally a Japanese healing technique, Reiki (which loosely translates to "spiritually guided life energy") treats patients—mentally, physically, emotionally, and spiritually—by properly aligning the body's seven energy centers, or chakras, to achieve a serenity of balance.

Prior to applying such alternative modalities, a thorough practitioner prepares by entering into a state of solitude through prayer or meditation. During the treatment application, practitioners may allow their intuition to guide them in their work; many channel the energy of God, or a Higher Power, by serving as a conduit through which the healing force flows. For example, during Reiki, a trained practitioner employing a non-touching technique uses intuition to guide her hands just above the recipient's body, intently focusing on an area in need of healing. This isolated healing may last several minutes before proceeding to another targeted area of the body. A dozen or more hand positions may be used in a traditional treatment session, which might last between 45 to 90 minutes, but localized treatments, such as concentrating on an injury, might take 20 minutes.

Persons who use complementary healing alternatives, such as Reiki, instead of conventional medical practices are not legally accountable to any standardized training or certification process, although it is generally acknowledged that training is required for each level of advancement, which ranges from that of apprentice, for personal use and working on others (Reiki I and Reiki II), to Master level at which point the training of others may take place.

Reiki has been shown to have a soothing effect on some individuals with autism. Tricia, mother to son, Nicholas, shared one such experience.

> When Nicholas was about 3 years old, I heard of a "Reiki Circle" for children with special needs. After calling to make the arrangements, I quickly learned that the entire family was encouraged to attend. The philosophy was when you have a child with special needs then it affects the entire family. So my husband, my daughter, my son, and I all went to The Place for Reiki to participate in this Reiki Circle. When we arrived, we went into a room filled with Reiki practitioners, all of which were strangers to my son Nicholas. At this point in his life, Nicholas was still very difficult to slow down. He often wanted to run around and was not able to sit still for more than a brief moment. When the practitioners began to send Reiki to us, we asked Nicholas to sit as there were candles lit around the room. He did sit and

actually laid on his back. His language at this age was very minimal and he could only say *more*, *go*, *eat*, and *juice*. The rest of the time he cried, screamed, tantrumed, and used his self-soothing techniques.

During this Reiki session, which only lasted 15 minutes, he told me, *"Eat!"* As I appreciated his communication, I told him it wasn't time to eat. He responded "Eat chicken nuggets...Wendy's!" I could not believe what I was hearing; not only did he use more than one word, he said words I *never* heard him say before. I said, "Honey, when we are done here we will get you chicken nuggets from Wendy's."

A few days passed and, while he had not uttered those wonderful words again for at least a year, he did bring me the business card for The Place for Reiki. As he handed me the card he said "Go." At first I was in shock! He had never made such a clear communication with me aside from the few words in his vocabulary. As I looked at the card I noticed it had a distinct picture of the stained glass from the entrance door. It occurred to me he recognized the picture from the front door. He wanted to go there again!

I must confess my past ignorance of such techniques. I hadn't had any direct involvement with this type of healing until about 2003 when I was staying in Ohio for several days making presentations for an agency that served children and adults with autism. The evening of my first day there, I hosted a small gathering of agency staff in my hotel suite to talk about their progress. Having been on my feet for eight hours prior, I was feeling a bit drained until one of the women there offered to perform Reiki on me. I was skeptical and suggested that she could try it, but I didn't expect much of anything. She positioned herself on the floor at my feet, and held her hands just above my moccasins. Within moments, I felt warmth permeate my feet reminiscent of propping them up in front of an open fireplace—it was really quite something! With a shy smile, my friend assured me that she had been properly trained and wasn't surprised in the slightest.

NATURAL-BORN HEALERS

But what if similar procedures came *naturally* to some—a byproduct of being inherently gentle and exquisitely sensitive? Ordinarily such individuals may be referred to as medical intuitives, possessing the innate ability to route out the source of pain or physical conflict sans medical training. Is it probable that certain individuals with autism have a natural healing aptitude unrecognized even by themselves as anything extraordinary for its divine capacity? Further, what if those individuals were, as a matter of happenstance, practicing the art of intuitive healing that, like my friend Kevin, went unrecognized by others? A situation much like the incident I witnessed with Kevin was told to me by Melissa, a support professional to a boy with autism, with whom I once worked.

> The boy is 3 years old and non-verbal aside from some short words that are beginning to be mumbled through a pacifier that his mother can't seem to keep out of his mouth. I have been over there many times, and the boy would come and hug me and jump on me to give him a piggy-back ride. He had never been aggressive with me. One day I had slept on my leg wrong and my knee was hurting me. It was a nice, sharp pain that I felt whenever I bent my knee slightly. (I always have had knee problems though.) I was sitting on the couch and the boy was running in circles, kind of like an airplane with his arms out like he was flying. He stopped suddenly and looked at me and headed over to me. He stood in front of me and put his arm up in the air with his hand clenched in a fist. I didn't move, and, since he had never done this before, I wasn't worried he would hurt me. He then hit me in the knee with his fist once. After he did it, he stopped and looked at me again before he hit the same spot on my knee a second time. I then realized that the pain that had been there was gone. I thanked him and he went back to flying like an airplane!
>
> Another time, with the same child, I was talking with his mother and he came over to me and laid the top of his body over my lap. He then looked up at me (made

eye contact) and said "baby." I thought I might be hearing things because when you're pregnant it seems like you hear sounds like "baby." But he repeated it twice more, turning away from me to continue playing with his toys. His mother said it sounded like he said "baby." I agreed. It was then that I told her my news. I was only three-and-a-half months along so I wasn't showing yet.

Tricia told me of another instance involving her son, Nicholas:

Nicholas has developed the ability to communicate with Bonnie [his practitioner] without any language barrier during their Reiki sessions. During one Reiki session he told Bonnie that he could help his daddy with the pain in his finger. Nicholas then went on to give specific details about his dad's finger and how sorry he felt for him and how much it must hurt. He said my husband should protect his finger in case he [Nicholas] jumps around and moves his arms, as he often does, so he won't accidentally bump his dad's finger and cause any more pain. When Bonnie called to give me the information Nicholas had explained to her, she had no prior knowledge that my husband, Randy, had caught his finger in a sander days before and was in extreme pain. Even she was amazed at what Nicholas had communicated to her.

THE VALUE OF "STIMMING"

In addition to exploring the concept of entrainment, I have previously written about the *value* of the self-soothing or self-regulating techniques of many persons with autism that, like Melissa's client and Nicholas in the preceding anecdotes, shows in repetitive rocking, twirling, hand-flapping, or vocalizing. These are diagnostic indicators of autism's clinical perseverations commonly called "stimming," which is usually categorized as a mindless, purposeless stereotypic behavior to be forcibly extinguished. (Interested readers should avail themselves of Donnellan and Leary's classic 1995 study, *Movement Difference and Diversity in Autism/Mental Retardation*, Madison, Wisc.: DRI Press.) However, in *Autism and the God Connection*, I correlate the outcome of autistic repetitious activities—which can increase serotonin production leading to states of altered consciousness—with *identical* activities deliberately engaged for spiritual gratification by those of religious standing: Gregorian chants, reciting the Rosary, the ecstasies of the whirling Sufi dervishes, shamanic drumming ceremonies, and the rhythmic rituals of certain tribes. It is incongruent that such spiritual repetition equals *mantra*, but autistic repetition equals *stimming*. If we are presuming intellect, there is no difference between the two, *and* the product of each activity would achieve the same outcome. Imagine my validation when author Oliver Sacks (*Awakenings*), professor of Clinical Neurology at Columbia University, also identified this concept in his 2007 book, *Musicophilia* (Alfred A. Knopf).

Sacks tells of a man of average intelligence who has dyskinesia, a movement disturbance, which manifested in tics that seized his body: mighty expulsions of breath and loud but unintelligible verbalizations, accompanied by muscle contractions that gripped his body and caused it to bow in synchronization. Throughout the course of his observations, however, Sacks discerned a rhythmic melody to his client's murmuring vocals and increasingly repetitive movements such that it took on the appearance of *davening*, a form of Hebrew prayer; indeed, Sacks identified language consistent with Hebrew, which his client confirmed, though unable to account for its random use. Still, Sacks's client reported a sense of contribution rather than affliction, the impetus of which was his melodic ritual. This culminated in an instance of entrainment witnessed by Sacks:

> Wanting to document this extraordinary scene, I went one day to the hospital with my tape recorder. As soon as I entered, I could hear Mr. R. down the hall. But when I entered the room I found a Sabbath service in progress. The cantillation was coming not from my patient, but from the davening rabbi himself. With the rabbi, presumably, the rhythmic emphasis of prayer had led to a sympathetic rhythmic movement of the body—but with Mr. R., it had happened the other way round. Not originally a man attracted to cantillation or prayer, he had now been drawn to this through the physiological accident of dyskinesia.

In the anecdote recounted by Oliver Sacks, the movements and vocalizations of the rabbi were veritably indistinguishable from that of his client once the two were conjoined in harmony. It would be fascinating to forecast the spiritual byproduct for each man should they have been so engaged on a regular schedule, and whom it would benefit as a result.

UNDISCIPLINED ENERGY

Not only do we require a re-envisioning of autism's perseverations, we must also acknowledge the purpose such rhythmic pulsations may hold as it relates to identifying and healing the physical energy of those held dear. Readers of *The Soul of Autism* will recall Ashtyn, an animal whisperer, with the ability to identify and feel the pain of animals. Her mother explained to me that when Ashtyn's puppy, Skippy, was injured by another child, the family thought that the dog had a broken leg (since he put a little pressure on it.) They decided to wait it out and see but the puppy cried and howled during the night. The following morning, they took Skippy to the vet and sat with other dogs and animals in the waiting area. Ashtyn reportedly kept staring at one dog in particular that seemed very tired. Ashtyn told her mother to take Skippy outside the vet clinic because "he" was afraid that he would be getting a shot. Though Ashtyn's mother reiterated that Skippy was only there for a check up, the dog ended up getting a shot! (Incidentally, Skippy only had a sprain.)

The brown dog Ashtyn had been staring at was there for a check up as well, but the dog also had Parvo disease, which is ultimately fatal. (As the family was leaving the clinic, Ashtyn remarked to her mother that the brown dog was terribly sad and had no words for her.) Not only did Ashtyn predict that Skippy required an unanticipated inoculation, she had asked her mother to take him outside. What's intriguing about this is that Parvo is contagious. Now, Ashtyn did not know this, but one wonders if she felt the other dog's pain, or heard something she just did not share. Further, was she trying to prevent Skippy from catching Parvo from the other dog? Ashtyn cried as she left the clinic, telling her mother that she did not want her dog to die. Her mother reports that Ashtyn is learning about emotion from her dog.

When Ashtyn had horseback riding lessons, the instructor warned her mother privately about a very thin horse they had received that was rescued from abuse; due to it being starved, it was very frail and weak looking. The instructor was afraid that this would upset Ashtyn but, instead, Ashtyn rushed to the stall and looked at the horse, never letting on about its condition. After her lesson and before leaving, Ashtyn had wandered off. They found her in the stall with the frail horse, perched on a stool and stroking the animal's head. Ashtyn's teacher beamed and remarked that this horse was very scared of people, and did not usually allow others to touch him at all. All were taken with Ashtyn's horse mothering. Ashtyn pet his face and told her mother that the horse's bones were protruding. On the drive home, Ashtyn observed that horses like her a lot because she makes them feel better—just like good medicine!

A caution exists for persons like Ashtyn who are natural-born healers and are also undisciplined in harnessing their empathic energies. Those individuals on the autism spectrum who are inherently gentle and exquisitely sensitive cannot help but to be so deeply affected by their intuitive perceptions of others that it may seriously disturb them, causing those individuals to react in an extreme manner. Even if anger, conflict, or duress is not directed at those individuals it may well affect them just as if it had been. An insensitive or unknowing caregiver might, in turn, completely misinterpret the causation and, instead, mislabel any such outpourings as stereotypical behaviors rather than discerning the true source. For example, Leesa, mother to son Zach, told of a typical reaction:

> I received a call today that my uncle (my father's younger brother) was taken to the hospital at about 12:30 p.m. By the time I got to my parents' house, we received the call that he had passed away. He had just completed his second chemotherapy treatment for lung cancer, and last week he told my dad that he never felt better. Interestingly enough, Zach was at day camp today and the note I received when he came home read as follows: "Zach began sobbing during lunch today for no apparent reason. It lasted for about five minutes. I asked him if he was okay and he signed 'yes,' and then he stopped crying. I just wanted to let you know because this is the first time he cried in day camp all summer."

Jamie, another mom, indicated concern for her son Trevor's empathic yet boundless capacity:

One of my recent surgeries was on my back. I was told I would be in the hospital for probably four days. However after my surgery I felt great! I wanted to walk that night, but they wouldn't let me. They made me wait until the next day and finally said I could go home. I was even cleared to go to my family's home to eat Thanksgiving dinner nearly less than 24 hours after my surgery! Trevor, my husband, and our other son, Ryan, picked me up from the hospital and we went to my grandmother's home for dinner. I felt awesome! It was really surprising to everyone, and everyone shrieked in terror when, out of habit, I scooped my niece up into my arms.

Then the dinner took a sad tone when we noticed Trevor cowering in a ball in the corner. He is usually so playful and cheery at grandma's home. He refused to eat and was white as a ghost. He kept saying things like, "Mommy does your back hurt?" and "Mommy, is your back better?" but he really would not talk at all other than that. He was shaking and a mess for an hour-and-a-half. We tried everything. Finally, my bandage was bothering me and my grandmother took it off, and Trevor came over to look at my incision. From that point on he started to talk and eventually ate. But he remained pale and displayed more "autistic tendencies" in the days to follow.

On December 1, he went to see his specialist in Pittsburgh and my husband explained this chain of events. The doctor said it was very clear what was happening. He was positive Trevor was healing me—and our eyes were opened to this. The doctor talked to Trevor about his energy, and how he was in need of getting big and strong, and to try to keep his energy for him. He told my husband that we needed to keep Trevor from healing because it was depleting his immune system and he was "a very sick little boy." And he was. The doctor said that Trevor was not channeling the energy, but using his own.

So from this time on, we have really tried to explain to Trevor about his gifts and how they are good, but we need him to grow and get big. But, Mr. Stillman, he is only 5 years old! He doesn't seem to understand us. I know you say "always presume intellect," and that is a very, very strong message to me. I have really taken that to heart and I know Trevor is having so much more to offer than what this world, or I, can take in. But I feel so inadequate to be his mom! I actually was doing my physical therapy stretches and he was helping me by sitting on my backside while I did my pushups (my physical therapist explained that this was a good way to help keep the pelvis down and the boys love to help mommy with my exercises), and I could feel this *incredible sensation*! It is impossible to put into words. It was like I was entering this warm, calm water. I was surrounded with love and beauty. It was like a place. And there was no pain. And all of the sudden I realized that Trevor was healing me again. Only this time I did not have the pain medications in me and I felt it!

I hope you don't think that this sounds "out there." We live in a small town and things like this just aren't really heard of. I am worried about Trevor being sick from using his healing, but we have no guidance in the matter. His doctor in Pittsburgh is wonderful, however, he has more than 400 families waiting to get in to see him. Plus, that is two hours away. I read your books *Autism and the God Connection* and *The Soul of Autism* and they helped me so much. I really felt alone before reading the books.

A Remedy

It is remarkable to me that Jamie's physician was innovative enough to advise her about Trevor's healing capacity—remarkable yet progressive! In 2009, I was, myself, invited to join an integrative medicine group that met on the campus of a prestigious and nationally-renown medical center located just a few miles from my home. The group was comprised of an ever-growing roster of holistic practitioners in varied disciplines, and the group's purpose was to slowly-but-surely

influence the medical center's old guard administration into informing the up-and-coming med students about alternative methods. The
group's efforts culminated in an on-site fair for the students by which
they could balance their traditional training with exposure to lesser-
known practices such as acupuncture and homeopathy. Concurrently,
I had begun learning of similar subset groups gathered at hospitals
scattered across the country in response to consumer demand, and
I was reminded of my vision in *The Soul of Autism* for the potential
of natural-born intuitives to become medical partners in some future
era—and remunerated with compensation commensurate with their
M.D. counterparts.

Because many—not all—people on the autism spectrum think in
terms of visuals, and are literal thinkers and learners, communicating
significant concepts in writing (and also in pictures for the very young)
is one manner of solidly reinforcing a given idea in order for it to be
retained and recalled. For example, I am not intelligent in a traditional
sense, and in academic settings I struggled to comprehend information
that was expressly didactic, or verbal. However, I am able to call up
minute details pertaining to specific persons and events stretching back
to near infancy—triggered by associated colors, activities, and emotions;
given adequate process time, I can identify people from decades prior
once I match their face with my internal Rolodex.

To explain the concept of natural-born healing and the importance
of not draining one's self empathically, I have composed a short narrative that may be used to counsel one so sensitive. It is to be read with
that person (or with her reading to you) on a regular basis until the
person demonstrates her understanding by adjusting her conduct to suit
the narrative's expectations. The routine may then be faded completely
once comprehension is assured.

My Gift of Healing
Part One

I have a gift of healing.

This means that when someone hurts, I feel it too.

I feel it because I am a very sensitive person.

This is called being an *empath*.

It is okay to feel upset for someone else.

When this happens, I can show them that I am sorry for how they feel. I can do this by_____.

This is called *compassion*.

Because I am a very sensitive person, I have to be careful.

I will try not to let someone else's hurting upset me too much.

If someone else's hurting upsets me too much, I may not be able to think about anything else. I may not be able to do anything else. I may become very emotional.

I will try to remember that it is their pain for them to feel. It is not my pain.

I can still show them compassion without feeling their pain as my own pain.

Part Two

My gift of healing also means that I can help others who are feeling pain.

I may do this by finding the pain and making it better. This is called *healing*.

I may do this by touching the area of pain.

I may do this by picturing the pain.

Or I may do this by praying about the pain.

Because I am a very sensitive person, it is important that I not try to heal all by myself.

If I try to heal all by myself, I may make myself feel very weak or even sick.

Before I try to heal someone, I will ask _____ [insert God, angels, saints, or other religious/spiritual sources] for help. I will ask that _____ [insert God, angels, saints, or other religious/spiritual sources] work with me to help heal.

If I do this, I should still be able to heal and feel okay afterward.

HEALING IN PRACTICE

Examples to support the preceding narrative may also be shared with the person on the autism spectrum—it is always validating to know one is not alone. Here is some anecdotal information that may prove useful. Regarding the spiritual support of angels and healing, Sarah, mom to Joseph, told me of the following manifestations:

> [Joseph] told me, in a general discussion about angels recently, that one visited him when he was ill (with a pretty bad and very sudden chest infection) in Spain. He was only about 2-1/2 at the time; we had not mentioned his illness to him since then. Thinking back, and medicine aside, he did make a miraculously fast recovery. He said she was sparkly and light, and had light hair and gave him a hug and made him better. He said the same one visited him in the hospital when he was a baby too (he had meningitis when he was nine months old and was in hospital for a while, critically ill). He also told me there was a baby in my tummy when I

was only two weeks pregnant and had no intention of telling him so early. He also talks about relatives he has never met and tells us the color of their cars, and so on.

Concerning one method of healing visualization, Ursula said that her teenage son Singen, "feels a desire to help people...he feels like he can absorb other's negative emotions to help calm them down and then he throws away that negative emotion. I've heard of that being done by shamans in Mexico. It surprised me to have him come out one day and tell me about it."

An example of laying-on-of-hands and healing by physical touch is shared by Justine, mom to son Able:

> I cannot remember when Able's ability to heal manifested itself. He actively began to use it when he was a teenager, particularly when on the football field and team members suffered minor injuries. However, when he was in his early 20s, I woke up unable to breathe with an asthma attack. I could not even get to the phone to call for help. Neither of us can recall how we came to be sitting on the couch together, but I do remember experiencing excruciating pain and then nothing at all. My first thought was I had died. I was truly enjoying the experience, the freedom from pain and the gentleness of my surroundings, when I felt a searing heat in my chest. I was back and my breathing was normal. Able's hands were on my ribs and his forehead gleamed with sweat. "I'm tired," he said. "You are alright. Go to bed."

It is vital that each individual with autism and healing capacity receives information of the same type and degree as anyone *neurotypical,* so as to be informed with clarity and elucidation. One way to establish a foundation of mutual understanding is to employ the written narrative indicated here; other opportunities may present themselves online, through local classes or courses, or by locating a trained mentor willing to aid the person with autism to gently tame and refine their abilities. If we do not presume the intellect of each person by providing such information, we may perpetuate that person's great apprehension for being without an explanation of their intimate and conceivably overwhelming experiences. We may also contribute to the very physically and emotionally draining aftermath that can be a byproduct of the undisciplined empathic healer. As noted, this emotional outpouring may lead to a litany of misinterpreted behaviors, such as acute anxiety and nervousness, sleeplessness, hyperactivity, and the inability to calm and focus. The proactive approach will likely be a *process*, and you may wish to learn more about healing and energy work as it pertains to your loved one with autism by contacting appropriate university and hospital staff, identifying wellness centers in your vicinity, searching the Internet for viewing material, or reading relevant reference works accessible through your local library.

A PREDISPOSITION FOR HEALING

It is an ironic prospect to discuss the healing potential of some individuals with autism when so much is being written about the race-against-time of which some parents and professionals feel compelled to partake in order to heal autism itself to, in essence, *heal the healers!* (Not only that, I am aware of New Age practitioners with little-to-no working knowledge of autism that have also made it their mission to "heal" autism, implying that there's something woeful to ameliorate.)

The healing potential of which I write may not necessarily show through more spectacular instances such as those related here. Oftentimes it shows in subtle, everyday examples of unexpected gifts, gains, and insights so frequently recounted to me by those moms and dads whose eyes have been opened to the profound learning opportunity presented by virtue of parenting the child with autism. I do not wish to invalidate those parents who desire the most advantageous future for their child—affecting a replica of normalcy that passes as acceptable by societal standards—but behavioral conditioning risks eradicating an individual's sense of authentic personhood. It also risks weaning away the sensitivities that contribute to that authenticity, as appears to be the case for one observant mother who remarked in an online blog (with my italics added for emphasis), "I have experienced similar [extraordinary] situations with my son. *They seem to have lessened in frequency as his autism symptoms improved.* In fact, I don't think we've had any unusual occurrences in many months. I have no idea if I was just dealing with coincidences and/or reading too much into things or if there is indeed a superior level of sensitivity involved. His teachers last year even made comments about his ability to know what they were going to say before they said it."

The autistic symptoms to which this mother refers likely include self-soothing techniques, such as hand-flapping, twirling in place, or repetitious vocalizing, in addition to perceived overreactions to sights, sounds, and textures that are aversive. But personally speaking, I wouldn't want to be entirely voided of my acute sensitivities, and it's terrifying to think of someone (such as well-intentioned parents) making that determination on my behalf. Perhaps a truce is in order for finding fair and reasonable compromise—allowing private moments for people with autism to *be autistic*—in lieu of the herculean efforts required to suppress and pass for normal all day long. Trust me, the world *hurts*, and passing for normal is an art form worthy of Academy Award consideration. One hypothesis recently proposed explains the painful clash experienced by many children and adults with autism in their attempts to assimilate with the world. Its contentions may offer an additional perspective to temper a balance of approach for one's superior level of sensitivity, and underscores the healing potential of those most emotionally attuned.

INTENSE WORLD SYNDROME

The October 15, 2007 online edition of *Frontiers in Neuroscience* presented intriguing research from the Brain Mind Institute, Ecole Polytechnique Fédérale de Lausanne, Switzerland, pertaining to individuals with autism and their environmental and social perceptions. "The Intense World Syndrome—An Alternative Hypothesis for Autism" by Henry Markram, Tania Rinaldi, and Kamila Markram, is among the fleeting minority of clinical studies to propose that the internal struggle so many persons with autism experience in reaction to external environmental conflict (crowds, traffic, and other sensory-assaultive stimuli), due to hyperactive sensory processing, may actually preclude their ability to conjoin with the world, causing them to, instead, withdraw and become socially isolative thus concealing their true intellectual gifts and talents (hence the study's title). The study's conclusions bear remarkable similarity to my own conjectures about human potential as regarding to the unlimited possibilities offered by many of our most gentle and sensitive citizens.

> The Intense World Syndrome suggests that the autistic person is an individual with remarkable and far-above-average capabilities due to greatly enhanced perception, attention,

and memory. In fact it is this hyper-functionality, which could render the individual debilitated. This perspective of hyper-functionality offers new hope for pharmacological as well as behavioral treatments. For example, while most of the commonly prescribed medications try to increase neuronal and cognitive functioning, we conclude that the autistic brain needs to be calmed down, learning needs to be slowed, and cognitive functions need to be diminished in order to re-instate proper functionality. In terms of behavioral treatments, the hyper-plasticity offers an immense scope for rehabilitation therapies that are based on excessive positive reward and comforting approaches and that avoid direct punishment, which may lead to a lockdown of behavioral routines. It may well turn out that successful treatments could expose truly capable and highly gifted individuals.

(To clarify, "successful treatments" for a person with autism, in this author's opinion, need to begin with the presumption of intellect; seeking redemption through an apology made directly to the offended individual whose intellect has not been presumed; identifying his or her most passionate topics of interest from which to develop age-appropriate curricula, meaningful relationships, and potential vocations; and discerning viable communication alternatives to speech, for each individual without a voice, with a belief that he or she can already read, and has important contributions to offer the world.)

In advancing its progressive twist, the Intense World Syndrome also purports that the "lack of social interaction in autism may therefore not be because of deficits in the ability to process social and emotional cues as previously thought, but because a subset of cues are overly intense, compulsively attended to, excessively processed, and remembered with frightening clarity and intensity. Autistic people may, therefore, neither at all be mind-blind nor lack empathy for others, but be hyper-aware of selected fragments of the mind, which may be so intense that they avoid eye contact, withdraw from social interactions, and stop communicating." It is this hyper-awareness, including an acute—not absence of—empathy for others, called *enhanced emotionality* in the research, that portends the ability to employ spiritual gifts, such as healing others, as naturally-occurring adjuncts; byproducts of painfully intense sensory sensitivities so frequently associated in individuals with autism.

OVERWHELMED AND OVERCOME

The Intense World Syndrome theorizes that the brain of one who is autistic contains local neuronal circuits that are compromised by hyper-reactivity and hyper-plasticity leading to neuronal circuitry that produces excessive functioning (over-reactions) to a world so intensely perceived.

Intense World Syndrome research includes, with proper support-ing citations, evidence contrasting a hypo-functioning (meaning under-responsive) brain amygdala which, in present theories of autism, contends emotional, social, and environmental disengagement (no eye contact and poor social interactions), with the newly proposed *hyper-functioning* amygdale, which may poise the person with autism for overwhelming bombardment in identical circumstances. It is this excessive overload which, the study asserts, causes social withdrawal in avoiding assimila-tion of complex stimuli. (Remember, the world *hurts*.)

The study continues, "We, therefore, propose that the autistic per-son may perceive [his] surroundings not only as overwhelmingly intense due to hyper-reactivity of primary sensory areas, but also as aversive and highly stressful due to a hyper-reactive amygdala, which also makes quick and powerful fear associations with usually neutral stimuli. The autistic person may try to cope with the intense and aversive world by avoidance. Thus, impaired social interactions and withdrawal may not be the result of a lack of compassion, incapability to put oneself into someone else's posi-tion, or lack of emotionality, but to the contrary a result of an intensely if not painfully aversively perceived environment." It is these kinds of experiences, the researchers contend, that fuel a secondary symptom of so-called impaired social interaction and autistic isolative tendencies—mediated by a hyper-reactive and hyper-plastic amygdale—spawning from reactions of extreme fear and anxiety. This makes sense when one consid-ers the tremendous preponderance of individuals with autism who are diagnosed with anxiety disorder, depression, and post-traumatic stress disorder—most of which stems from a fear of the unknown and a helpless-ness for having no control, and most of which *we have created*.

The Intense World Syndrome, as a hypothesis to explain autistic hypersensitivity, is but one of hundreds of contributions to the field of ongoing autism research, yet it correlates well with anecdotal feedback from friends and acquaintances on the autism spectrum who report that emotion literally seizes hold of their bodies and jerks and contorts their limbs in response to people, places, and things. As the study succinctly observes, "Many of the observed neuropathologies can be viewed as a consequence of hyper-reactive and hyper-plastic neural circuits, while many of the autistic symptoms may be re-interpreted in the light of an aversively intense world." It may well be that this acute and painful sensitivity is what compels many people with autism to not only feel strong sensory reactions to an assaultive environment, but to also feel overcome with emotional extremes in ways that are uncommon and exquisite. This was precisely the question posed to me by Ziek, a mother worried for her daughter, Elena, when she e-mailed me in 2005 as I was researching my first book about autism and spiritual giftedness:

> Over the past months, two of her grandparents (my mother-in-law and my father) have had health crises and have been hospitalized or have otherwise had horrible nights of pain and/or fearful experiences. With my father, it was three nights that he was hospitalized in Florida, and with my mother-in-law (here in New York City) it has been several trips to the hospital, and chronic suffering with stomach cancer, bedsores, and generalized failure of the body's systems.

> *On every one of these occasions*, Elena (at a school in Pennsylvania) has awakened in the night at precisely the time of the crisis and has been wild and hyper until I, or someone there, connects her sleeplessness with the event and is able to explain to her what is happening and the treatment or care being provided, and that the grandparent is now resting or going home soon, or whatever. At that time she becomes totally focused and listens carefully; then she becomes somewhat calmer, but is still somewhat hyped up for another day or so, sometimes unable to stay in her classroom or at the meal table.

> This is not a new condition with her. She has a lifetime of very unreliable sleep patterns, always sensitive to community celebrations (the home team winning a big sporting event, New Year's Eve parties in town, etc.). And although she has *very* sensitive hearing, none of these have been where she would physically hear or be disturbed by the

hoopla, but she knows, nonetheless, and she doesn't go to sleep until the party's over. But this 100-percent-consistent pattern with these two grandparents is uncanny and we would like to provide her (and the others around her) any possible relief from this distress.

The relief comes from not only a sense of knowingness, but from understanding the connection that drives it. Mother and son, Mary Jane Gray Hale and Charles Martel Hale, Jr., write in their 1999 book, *I had no Means to Shout!*, of Charles's exceptional life. As an adult, Charles was believed to be "among the most disabled, non-productive consumers at the workshop [for the developmentally disabled]" and that his clinical evaluation categorized him as "severely or profoundly mentally retarded." However, that all changed once Charles learned to type and could reveal the truth of his intellect. His attitude speaks of grace, humility, and an extraordinary tolerance for his anguished predicament; but his expressions also speak to the capacity to heal not only himself, but others through the only emotion that is relevant under such conditions: love. To that end, Charles writes of his perspective in a composition for his mother, "I now feel better about myself in every way and I will try my very best to deserve all of the wonderful thoughts and prayers that have come my way. I will try all of my life to keep an uplifted attitude and to remember how much I was loved by you and Daddy and let that serve as an inspiration to try to help others as best I can. I have so much love for others and I sometimes think that is the reason I was born handicapped, just to let others know that they must live their lives with an uplifted spirit in order that it was not in vain for them to have been born in the first place."

The implications of bearing so much love for others—as does Charles and countless other autistics—and channeling that rarefied energy into healing others, holds limitless potential. If we can accept, embrace, and support those individuals to tame and refine their gifts as natural-born healers, new disciplines unfold to complement the burgeoning field of integrative medicine in tandem with medical, holistic, and homeopathic practitioners; the implications, then, for a future merging human giftedness at all levels of functioning is only just beginning to dawn.

PART TWO

MYSTERIOUS WAYS

Chapter 3

Impossible Gifts

"Only he who can see the invisible can do the impossible."
—Frank Gaines

In my two previous spiritually themed books, I have introduced some pretty far-out-there concepts, I must admit, though I always qualify any discussion of this topic by quoting an old cliché, "I don't make the news, I just report it." And there wouldn't be anything to report if unconventional experiences and extraordinary accounts of spiritual giftedness weren't transpiring for my readers beyond a select few. In fact, I not only hear regularly from people throughout North America, but internationally as well. This is an affirmation of my original contentions for pursuing this very delicate aspect of what gets perceived as a debilitating disease: to illuminate the truth about autism from a unique perspective.

As you may surmise, I have prevailed against campaigns of condemnation defaming my character, some of which have been quite vicious, but, historically, such has been the lot of those who advance progressive ideals. Where I've been criticized by naysayers, I find that they tend to be coming from one of several places:

* They are not open-minded to uncommon spiritual or religious occurrences.
* They have no firsthand, intimate knowledge of autism and only know what's been sensationalized as tragic by the media at large.

* They don't presume intellect in those with autism and believe such individuals are vacant, void, or "soulless."

* They are parents who have only their own very young child as their single point of reference, and, thus, their views are limited (whereas I have hundreds of individuals with autism as my point of reference).

* They are parents who don't recognize anything particularly spiritual about their own child so they unilaterally dismiss my theories.

Taking any of these positions doesn't make my dissenters wrong; we're just coming from very different viewpoints and will have to agree to disagree. In reviewing my writings, one blogger, who is also a parent, consistently references Penn and Teller, and James Randi—all of whom seek to expose hoaxsters that financially bilk unsuspecting persons through fraudulent trickery. However, I categorically reject the insinuation that I am of a reputation that is disingenuous and deliberately deceptive like such charlatans. (And to those who would question my credibility: if I were not, myself, authentic in who I am and what I do, I wouldn't have lasted 20 minutes in this field let alone well over 20 years.) I've also found that some parents in the latter two groups of the preceding list tend to struggle with my philosophies. They second-guess themselves because they may feel guilt or denial brought on by choices they've made in terms of *autism treatments* that, in hindsight, and in light of my philosophies of presuming intellect, may seem disrespecting of their child's capabilities. But this is remedied by appreciating the true, yet dormant, intellectual capacity of each person deemed inferior coupled with an understanding that there are many different kinds of intelligence beyond what is reflected in an IQ exam.

What I'm about to share next are some of the more unbelievable accounts I've received, much of which I have held in reserve for some years now before going public. I don't have measurable, efficacious evidence of these instances; only anecdotal testimony told to me in confidence, much of it from people whose reputations I can personally vouch for. But, for the sake of being thorough and complete, I am including this information here. The reader may draw his or her own conclusions as to the viability of these accounts, and temper this information with one's own background, knowledge, and beliefs about human potential.

THE UNIVERSE OF THOUGHT

Those among us who are average or *neuro-typical* tend to find difficulty relating to the plight of many autistics—being without a voice and living in silence. Too often the average person is focused on gratifying and satiating physical needs throughout each day: creature comforts pertaining to food and drink; temperature; toileting and bathing; sexual satisfaction; material and financial acquisitions; and personal appearance (and acceptance by others of such) for example. Outside of those who consciously devote time to prayer or meditation, often overlooked are opportunities to isolate in absorbing states of solitude and reflection. But such conditions are *natural* to many people with autism for whom the physical body is alien—a leaden vessel at odds with a high-frequency identity that continually ponders aesthetics and high-thought. It is not unlike a perpetual meditation—always thinking, observing, processing, and contemplating.

Because most human beings are oriented with an emphasis on the physical, it may be very challenging to consider a reversal in orientation that emphasizes the cerebral over the corporeal. In the same way that people continually seek to fulfill their physical needs as a natural aspect of being human (with a minor percentage of that time, by comparison, accountable for states of solitude), comparable needs are required for fulfillment intellectually in ways that are expansive and unlimited by those for whom the physical doesn't work. Our orientation to the physical, which is tangible and measurable, makes it difficult to accept realms of thought that are intangible and usually unquantifiable.

But the universe of thought and aesthetics and creation is vast, attainable by anyone desiring to access it. In fact, there are those among us who make a determination to access it *deliberately* by endeavoring to effect the shift in orientation of which I write, creating what I've coined the *dichotomy of consciousness*. These citizens are not autistic and yet they attempt to replicate an autistic experience the majority of the time! They seek to free themselves of the extraneous stimuli of crowds, telephones, radio, television, and incessant social chatter. Instead, they spend as much time as possible in silence, but it is silence with a purpose. The intended purpose is the incremental achievement of enhanced enlightenment that comes of such states of solitude. It comes in thoughts and images and icons and revelations not usually afforded to those of us for whom much time is focused on gratifying physical needs. Just who are these characters that willfully *choose* to behave in a manner virtually identical to the person with autism? As previously noted, they are the nun, the monk, the yogi, the guru, and the priest. If we presume the full intellectual competence of those with autism, there is *no* difference in the outcome of the same pensive rituals enacted by these individuals; indeed, the autistic one may be more *advanced* for naturally being born into a way of being that those of revered religious and spiritual standing—whom we tend to elevate and glorify—desire to *emulate*!

My friend, Wally, is a person with autism who also experiences ALS, or Lou Gehrig's. Wally used to be able to type his thoughts and feelings but, in its progressive stages, his deteriorating neurology contests his limbs, rendering them immobile. He presently communicates using a laser device that tracks his eye gaze directed at a computer screen, or by typing with some physical support. Wally has written of being present with an intellect intact, and spending grand amounts of time replaying and reviewing life events, weighing in his mind the postulations, conjectures, and contradictions of any given circumstance. Living life in silence has granted Wally perspectives not unlike theories of perception.

> My reality might be different from yours even though I am experiencing the same stimuli as you are. Ten people can look at the same painting and each person will experience it differently. Each person's reality will be different when looking at the painting. The painting that each of the people sees is exactly the same one, however each person's reality when viewing the painting is unique. Telling one of the other viewers the ideas that the painting evoked in you is sharing your reality, at the moment, with another person.
>
> Reality, as you experience it, is linked to your past experiences, therefore the reality that you experience and express to another person is in the realm of one's mind. One looks to the occasional thought that passes through one's mind and wonders if this is reality or is it fantasy. Perhaps I am your thought and you are mine. To you, when

you see me in person, I am real, not a thought; to me you are the same. Years ago, when you saw me in person, I was real, but now you think of me as a mere thought. I am a thought to you now as you think of me.

Wally's position enables him the valuable opportunity to explain to the layperson the benefits of dwelling in solitude, the potential outcomes of which compare, or exceed, the identical existence of those who deliberately enter into silence.

I still do not understand war, killing, racism, and political ambitions that lead to the domination of other people. To me, these concepts rarely delineate any clear thinking on the part of those responsible for such actions. In my thinking, in my world, there is no room, nor place, for war, killing, violence, or domination…. Living in my world, there is total love, acceptance, and equality between all that is living.

The mind, once it is unleashed from its human bondage, is free to ponder reality in dimensions yet to be proven, on levels unheard of, and with unlimited understanding. In each thinking-person's mind there is, amounting to this realization, the potential for infinite love and understanding of this power that each of us has but seldom recognizes. Reaching our full mental potential to become this rational establishes that our understanding of our world would then be very nearly complete. Years ago I wanted to be "normal." Now, I think that I am "normal" and the rest of the world is not.

Wally's dimensions of thought yet to be proven compels us to wonder: does one journey alone in such dimensions or do our paths intersect with others on the journey? And if our paths intersect with others, might they also *intercept* and *interfere*? The idea of intrusive, unwanted thinking (in the form of remote-distance mind control) then takes on a whole new meaning as we traverse the galaxy of our collective capacity.

MIND GAMES

A number of years ago I was contacted by Maya, a music thera-pist and gifted musician, with whom I had become acquainted through monthly gatherings of people on the autism spectrum who lived in silence yet communicated by alternative means such as by typing or by using specialized equipment called assistive technology. Maya knew of my spiritual research as it related to autistics of all age ranges, and e-mailed me in desperation mode; her predicament pertained to the concept of interfering thoughts projected by one individual to others. In particular, Maya was finding that some of her music therapy ses-sions with autistic clients were being waylaid by the intrusive agenda of another individual with a powerful telepathic clutch that disrupted the interactions between Maya and her clients with the equivalent of white noise, static, or contrary conduct.

I followed up with Maya by phone, and she was relieved to find someone with whom she could speak of such matters openly, freely, and with unconditional acceptance. Based upon what Maya was telling me, the situation was escalating to the point of becoming destructive. The circumstances involved the apparent ability of Roy, an adult with autism, to hold mental thrall over another adult with autism, Helen, whom I had also met previously, as well as others. Maya and I discussed a number of options, and here, in her own words direct from our e-mail exchanges, she summarizes the sequence of events that took place. I am hopeful that perhaps Maya's struggle will have relevance for some readers of this book.

> I have promised Helen that I would ask you for help in a matter concerning Roy. He continues, unfortunately (or fortunately, I suppose, depending on how I happen to be choosing to view the situation at any given time), to inter-fere in music therapy sessions (particularly with Facilitated Communication users, possibly with others) as well as in my friendship with Steven (who does use FC). Since taking a break from Roy wasn't working at all, because, as I said, he never took a break—just kept interfering in a more intense way with the folks I support—I went back to work with him in mid-April.

None of the folks I work with have been able to "stop" him from (apparently) creating a lot of "noise" while they are with me and "getting them" to behave in unusual ways (that is, wanting to leave when it is someone who usually hates to leave sessions, becoming physically violent, etc.), and I have no words of wisdom to offer them (at least from the perspective of getting someone to "go away"). The idea of creating a prayerful space never really took hold for any of them.

I have tried reminding them that they have the power to choose whether or not to act on what he is saying (or whether or not they want to listen or to give any of it meaning). This has been somewhat effective for Tony [another client] and for Helen. Helen (and Tony), however, have continued to tell me "he is very loud," "he won't stop," and Helen literally spends the entire session "fighting" with Roy. It's a bit...well, whacky. I told her that I would ask if you had any advice as to how not to "hear" someone who is behaving in an invasive manner.

I, myself, continue to sense Roy very regularly. The difference, though, is that I now have a better ability to recognize when it's Roy "pushing" me to do something versus my own thoughts. I'm not 100 percent, but I'm a heck of a lot better at it than I was.

Well, I truly want to thank you for your written narrative explaining the situation. [To the reader: this narrative was originally developed to aid a friend and client of my own, Josh, and it accompanies Josh's story published in my book *Autism and the God Connection*. It is similar to the narrative from the "Art of Healing" chapter of this book.] I read it to both John [another client] and Helen today. John was (after a long period of refusing to use FC at all until Roy stops interfering) able to tell me he liked the idea of a written narrative, and it seemed to help him stay in touch with me while Roy (apparently) teased him in his mind. At least he was able to get his hitting at me under control (thank goodness). He had difficulty communicating with me, it seemed, but he was able to also convey in words (via FC) that he had to "go—Roy is bothering me." This was terrific progress for him. He has not been able to communicate his distress over this experience (although he has begun to make more use of the music to do so), and this was an important step for him. I found that I had to concentrate every ounce of focus I had on really aligning myself with the strength and peace within him. I'm not sure what helped in the end—I'm just glad that we seemed to feel more connected than we have for quite a frustrating while.

Helen was delighted to hear from you as always. She also loved the idea of a written narrative, but she was uncomfortable with the idea of God. We revised it together, and she was able to ask me to read it to her a number of times as Roy tried to force his voice through her hand [to type her thoughts]. She has really been a trooper. When he started to intrude she had terrible difficulty and was unable to resist his insistence that she speak for him at all. She now has developed a great determination to not have her voice or her time with me taken away (especially because this is the only time she has a voice because her regular support staff do not use FC with her).

What surprises me (still) is that Roy would feel the need to continue with this constant intrusion. It seems that no matter how much support he is offered he is unable to stop. I would agree with obsessive-compulsive disorder; however, he is receiving an awful lot of medication for his OCD, and—my gosh—what the heck else can a person do? He is even able to FC with at least one other person now (maybe more—I'll have to check in with his day staff).

At least it seems as if when I am geographically farther away, I don't feel as affected. I'm not sure whether it's because I'm farther away or if it's because I was busy at a conference. When I've gone to visit with my parents in Arizona, I also have had less of a sense of intrusion. Odd, and it makes me curious as to why it all seems more intense when I'm in my usual spaces. Hmmm.

I had an interesting, if completely confusing and hard to believe, conversation with my friend, Steven (who communicates via FC). The thing was that it was, possibly (?), allegedly (?) a conversation between Roy and his alter ego (for lack of information and/or a better way to describe it) on Sunday. Honestly, I am left confounded, and I'm concerned that researching all my old Roy notes (and I do have piles and piles of papers and notebooks related to sessions and conversations with him) is just going to keep him attached to me forever (that is, by keeping me hooked, so to speak).

Here is my question to you, Bill: are you able to tell, from your vantage point, whether or not Roy is lying, or if he is truly inhabited by a man named Gary and is being honest in telling me he needs help?

I just can't tell any more, and it seems to me that Roy has been not truthful with me from the instant he started to use FC with me. His most clear and accurate comments were first made to my friend, Lori, and he mentioned Gary to her then. His first comment about Gary was "Gary is not here," followed by his being in another building at the institution. Then he told Lori "Gary is Maya's former husband." Well, I do have a former husband, but his name is Tim, and he did work at the developmental center at the time.

Roy also made a lot of very outrageous claims to Lori, such as telling her he was going on a trip to Hawaii (while he lived in the institution), and dropping names of people who didn't seem to exist anywhere. I did not "hear" these types of comments from him. When he finally began to type clearly with me (after quite a long time, I might add), his comments were almost instantly sexualized and along the lines of "you marry me, Maya" (picture Maya throwing up her hands in general dismay and confusion and lack of clue).

To say the least, I have no idea where to go from here. He had a very rough time of things when he arrived at the developmental center, and he is not the youngster he was back then—quite a hellion, from what I've read in his old chart notes. On the other hand, who knows where all this sadistic stuff has come from? Well, as I've said before, I think chronic trauma has a tremendously debilitating effect on people's psyches (which is not a revelation of any sort, I'm sure), so it may just be the effects of extreme emotional pain and mental illness.

At any rate, I don't know whether engaging in dialogue with him (Roy/Gary) is a better idea or a worse one. I just can't tell. Truly, I don't think I feel as weary as I probably sound—just quite confused. I guess the best thing to do is to keep reminding myself that God is still (and always will be) way stronger than any ill will and rotten-eggishness in the world. Thank goodness.

I too shall pray, inviting Holy Spirit to help me remember the truth for myself, Roy, Gary, and my friend, Steven (as well as the rest of the crew). But, after much painful deliberation, I've decided I simply (at this point) need to stop working with Helen and the others. It's a very difficult decision, and, as a result, I'm feeling Roy's panic (I think—who knows? It could be mine as well). I guess you're right to be sort of worried. I truly don't have the emotional or physical energy to continue to go through this much longer. I don't know that it will help, because I believe Roy is disturbing other clients who don't use FC or speech as well. At this point, though, I can't be effective as their music therapist, and they aren't able to be (1) present or (2) make use of music therapy at all.

It's really quite difficult to say what exactly is going on—be it spirit possession or simply out of control fear and guilt. When I thought about things the other day, I pondered the possibility that Roy could be influencing my clients (and my friend, Steven, who alternates between appearing to be very upset and horrified by Roy's intrusions and feeling very aroused and sadistic when he is no longer able to "stop" him from interfering with his thoughts) through hypnotic means. Most of the folks I know tend to rock or perform various repetitive movements/sounds, and they're already, it seems, in a somewhat hypnotizable state. All Roy really has to do is suggest away, and they are virtually "enslaved" by him.

Either way, I think that my continued engagement is making this worse, and I need to find a way to completely disengage from Roy—even if it means no longer being able to serve the other folks I have worked with for so long. It saddens me no end, I must admit. Honestly, though, I can't justify putting either my clients or myself through this torment.

For me, personally, I will have to continue to examine my own thinking, my own fears and beliefs. I have been attempting to establish which thoughts are mine and which are "picked up" from elsewhere. It is very difficult to do, because I experience other people's feelings as if they're my own a lot of times. At least, I think I do. It's very odd, because I've never considered myself to be particularly attuned or sensitive in that sense, but it seems that I've gotten to be that way to some extent. Or I always was, and now I'm simply more aware of it.

No Easy Answers

Maya's circumstances were multilayered in complexity. Not only was she grappling with concerns for Helen and the others (Roy included), she was also coming to terms with her own heretofore unrecognized sensitivities—as an artist she is, perhaps, more open and naturally susceptible—and the capacity for her *own* thoughts to feel intruded upon such that she found herself questioning her own mental deliberations.

As for Roy, here is someone who, as Maya intimated, has a long history of institutional living which, as you'll recall from this book's introduction, is never pleasant but is, more often than not, traumatizing and dehumanizing. In someone autistic such as Roy, the impact of such treatment cannot be underestimated; it renders many to either explode or implode in surrender to symptoms indicative of mental illness. This seems to be the case for Roy, and aspects of grandiosity (symptomatic of the bipolar-manic phase) are evident in Maya's report when Roy discusses relocating to Hawaii, clearly impossible at the time; making sexual overtures; and suggesting that his alter-ego, Gary, was Maya's former husband. (Readers of *The Soul of Autism* will note great similarities between Roy and Vic, a case study included in that book.) Whereas many, like Roy, may become reactive in a *physical* manner by injuring themselves, harming others through acts of physical aggression, or destroying property, Roy is passive-aggressive in expression of his feelings of isolation, inequity, and a deeply wounded psyche; and he takes it out on others in a manner that is subtle, invasive, and deceptive given his orientation away from the physical in favor of the cerebral. In short, Roy is a psychic bully.

The disruptions seemingly perpetrated by Roy upon others, who are vulnerable and unable to resist, call into question the viability of legitimate mental health diagnoses in people so acutely and sensitively disposed. If Helen and the others so affected were, in fact, able to verbally self-report, just how would they respond to the standard psychiatric chestnut intended to route out schizophrenia, *"Do you hear voices?"* Hell, yes, they hear voices—*literally*—from the voices of nursing staff talking at the other end of the corridor (by means of autistic supersonic hearing) to the Roys of the world attempting to throw around their weight and exert their authority by playing mind games! (Read on for more about this clinical inconsistency in Part Three of this book.) It would not be the last time I'd learn of such sabotage and, in one instance, the intrusions were coming to a person with autism from another halfway around the world (in the universe of thought, physical distance is of no consequence).

It is the role of parents and caregivers, then, to help the healers; to lovingly and compassionately support them to understand and make *proactive* use of their spiritual gifts—if we can even discern them as such. I always advocate erring on the side of caution and courtesy rather than leaping to judgment about so-called aberrant behavior. If that had been Roy's case, he may have been spared the damage that prompted him to retaliate in a manipulation of entrainment principles gone awry. It is a misguided use of power, but attainment of power nonetheless, that causes one to impose a desperate authority at any cost. Conjoining in compassion is the call we must heed in order to appreciate the uprising *shift* with which we are faced.

CURIOUSER AND CURIOUSER

People often ask how what I write about is associated with Indigo kids, Crystal children, Rainbow kids, and the like—purported "new" kids with advanced skills, perceptions, and intelligence. To be honest, I don't have a clue. And, to be candid further, I have deliberately avoided reading about this movement. I mean no disrespect to the authors of such books, and I understand the correlations between what I talk about and the purported new kids, but I can't relate to it. Again, this should not be interpreted as a slight to my fellow authors (some of whom I have met), but I'm writing about people considered to have a *disability*, half of which are neurologically compromised and incapable of verbal communication, and at least 70 percent of whom are labeled mentally retarded. Still others are diagnosed with extreme forms of mental illness. I'm also not focused exclusively upon children, as is so often interpreted; I am well affiliated with adults with autism who have come forward to share their uncommon experiences, as well as the very young. What I can commit to is to state that there is, collectively, a growing appreciation for a shift that is occurring as it relates to our upcoming generations. We all want the world to be different, better, and tranquil, and who better than our young people to bear the mantle of responsibility and expectation for such a challenging aspiration. Remember, our role is to help the healers, to practice prevention techniques instead of intervention management, and to aid our loved ones to tame and refine their great gifts once we acknowledge them ourselves. This requires the authenticity of discernment.

Some years back, I received an anonymous e-mail from a parent with a worrisome concern: whenever her daughter with autism would become enraged and tantrum, the family's garage door would malfunction and spontaneously open and close. This mom wanted to know if the two occurrences were related and, if so, what to do about it. At the time I had never heard of anything so seemingly outrageous, and I was only just beginning to explore a connection between autism and spiritual giftedness. Although I didn't dismiss it entirely, it did sound outlandish and immediately conjured *Carrie* in my mind. But, by virtue of my reputation as "you're the only one who will understand," I've been appointed as the go-to guy for virtually anything out of the ordinary when it comes to autism. What this means is that, occasionally, I attract an outer fringe of followers who have a different reality than I do. For example, people have told me that a child with autism known to them is the second coming of Jesus Christ (this presents an obvious dilemma when more than one person is telling me the same thing). Or that people with autism are half-human and half-alien, an in-bred extraterrestrial race sent here to save the planet.

As unbelievable as some (or all!) of what I've recounted in now three autism-and-spirituality books may be for the average layperson, my intent has never been to unreasonably glorify anyone with autism in some polarized extreme—that is as much a disservice as the other extreme of dehumanizing and degrading the very same individuals. We are *all* more alike than we are different, and I'm merely illuminating aspects of a unique way of being so that we may learn of our collective potential as humankind from those who've already been there, done that, in terms of hypersensitivity and harvesting the ancillary fruits of such. To that end, I do believe that it is healthy to be skeptical though open-minded. Whatever became of the mom with the telekinetic kid? Apparently I didn't honor her report then in ways I might have now because I never saved the e-mail. Knowing what I know now, I'm starting to wish I had.

AN ELECTIC MIX

What follows is a mixed bag of sorts, bits and pieces of information passed on to me—usually by parents—that appear plausible enough to relay here. These anecdotes don't fall into the category themes I've already identified such as telepathy, premonition, animal communication, and the like; and, because I've chancing to reveal more of the iceberg's tip, I've withheld transcribing these accounts before at the risk of sounding too bizarre and completely dismantling any credibility. However, given the overwhelmingly positive reception to my writings, I'm venturing to further the cause in hopes that yet another family will not feel like they're the only ones experiencing something they can't readily explain.

In more than a few instances I've heard of a person with autism speaking fragments of a language unknown to them. This may be difficult to separate from the errant vocalizations that even those with autism may be unaware they are expelling, and which some with autism have, themselves, explained away as nonsense, nuisance, or irritating distractions not of their volition. Yet, in my book, *The Soul of Autism*, one extraordinary account came from the mother of a 14-year-old son with autism who is non-speaking. She wrote that, several years before, their family's church had a South American missionary visiting during one Wednesday evening service. In the middle of the missionary's relating details of his country and his work there, he suddenly ceased and gave a message in tongues. The mother's son, sitting beside her, repeated the missionary *word for word in the same language and as plainly as the missionary had spoken it*. She told me, "It seemed to be some sort of Native American dialect; there was no further interpretation, but everyone there was stunned."

Julia wrote of an example of her son Adam's remarkable aptitude for accessing a foreign language to which he had no prior exposure:

> Have you found in your work with some children, who are "non-verbal" but are vocal, that some of the things they say we cannot understand or think as gibberish, but others who are well-versed in foreign languages understand? For example, my brother-in-law was around Adam a lot over the holidays and knows some Portuguese from his missionary work that he does. There were quite a few instances where Adam would say something and my brother-in-law would say, "That means music in Portuguese." In these instances whatever Adam was saying was relevant in Portuguese to what he was doing. He was playing with a guitar and my brother-in-law heard the words *guitar* and *music* in

Portuguese. Have you heard of any other examples of this? No one in my family speaks this language, so I'm a little puzzled. Could this just be a weird coincidence or is this language very similar to ours in the way that some words could be sounding similar?

Similarly, Dawn, mother to a 24-year old man with Asperger's, wrote of another case of understanding an unknown language:

God has used my son to teach me to communicate and respect others, and the importance of advocacy and determination! And my son's insight into our Lord Jesus is phenomenal while his insight into the world is limited! Once while in church, someone was laying hands and speaking in tongues, and my son understood what was being said over each person, but when I asked about other times that people had spoken in "tongues," he said that they weren't saying anything at all (just as I had suspected!). Although he is very complex, he thinks in very simple terms. I love it! No deceit in him! I just wanted to connect with you for my son! Thank you for being there!

Tricia's son, Nicholas, used his ability to speak in tongues in order to intervene where healing was required:

When we went for our Reiki session, a family was just leaving as they finished their session. At the time I was distracted by signing in, but I noticed out of the corner of my eye Nicholas holding onto a man's hand. The man was bent down and talking to Nicholas. I assumed the man was a Reiki practitioner and that was why Nicholas was interacting with him. I made this assumption because he *never* willingly sought out physical contact with a stranger before this time. After a few minutes, I realized that Nicholas had a hold of this man's hand and was not letting go. He was trying to pull the man back into the room in which the Reiki is given. We tried to avoid this because there were rules that only one family is permitted at a time. This man and his family has just finished, so we kept trying to separate them so he could leave with his family. After several minutes of a struggle we physically got Nicholas into the room and the man left.

While in the room he was kicking at the door and kept saying "More." We decided to begin the Reiki session as another family would be coming and we only had 15 minutes. Bonnie, the owner, began the Reiki session and started to speak in one of her Native American languages. This didn't surprise me, as I have heard her do this many times before. As soon as she paused, the most profound thing happened. Nicholas began to respond back to her in the same type of Native American language. I could not believe what I was hearing. I was in absolute shock! The other Reiki practitioners at first thought this might have been normal for him because he was so relaxed as he spoke.

Nicholas and Bonnie had a few exchanges of this language and then she said, "Do you want to know what he said?" I immediately said, "Yes, tell me!" She said he told her that he wanted the man to come back into the room because he needed more healing. We were all amazed! A few months later we found out that the same man had a tumor on his brain. Sadly, he died just four or so months after having this profound experience with Nicholas. If we had only listened to what he was trying so desperately to communicate.

And, finally, Lucy writes:

I don't cry very often, and I never once cried about my son having autism ever since I first heard what the word meant. But tonight he said something he never has said before. "Leibes" is the closest I can come to what he said. I asked him what language that was from, and he said "Germany."

He is very speech challenged, or whatever the current term is for middle-to-low-functioning autism. He has had no exposure at all to German, and no exposure to spontaneous language development in any other language than English. I don't know what to make of it, or how to approach any sort of communication that is intuitive based on an experience which did not come rationally. He smiled at me like we both knew that nobody would believe us if we actually admitted that he expressed any kind of communication.

[Note that in follow up to Lucy's story, I contacted Michael Nagula, publisher of the German translations of my spiritual books. I asked him about the word *leibes* and here is his reply, "The word *leibes* is the genitive of leib, which means body or corpse. Nowadays we usually use the word *körper* (body, but not for dead people—that's a leiche or leichnam). Leib is more often used in biblical or spiritual contexts or in older German, like in "Der Leib Gottes," meaning the materialization/personification of God. There is another meaning inherent in the word *leib*. It can mean "vessel" as well if it's used in contexts regarding soul or spirit. When, for example, at the Last Supper Jesus broke the bread, he said (in our Bible editions): "This is the Leib of God."]

If there is an explanation for such spontaneous episodes, I would suggest that it has less to do with ESP or anything paranormal, and more to do with the harmonious, in-the-zone wavelengths that arise when we are entrained with one another—bonded in the moment in unconditional acceptance and understanding. It is in this same manner that we may be most apt to experience spiritual rapture when two or more are gathered together in worship.

AMAZING ACCOUNTS

In consideration of the next several anecdotes, one wonders if the principles of quantum physics don't come into play as partial explanation for what transpired, even though what's transpired may seem too incredible to believe. Or, are these tales simply additional accountings of individuals with autism unaware of the extraordinary nature of their own capacity? Michelle, a staff person whom I have mentored, contacted me with an unusual circumstance relayed to her by a family with whom she was consulting. I followed up with Pamela, mother of the family, who apprised me of the situation in her own words:

> My son got encephalitis when he was 5 years old. It started with a rash, the hiccups, and a very bad headache. He lost most of his language. He appears to be autistic. He is totally aware that he is different from how he used to be. He cries and says, "I want to talk! I want to talk!" He suffers a great deal. Every day it is painful to watch. Almost a year after he got sick, I begged God for a sign that he would recover.
>
> When my husband and I got married, we went to Rome for our honeymoon. My parents got us these special tickets for newlyweds to meet the Pope. We went to Pope John Paul II's Wednesday audience. We sat on stage with him and got introduced to him. We kissed his ring and he blessed our marriage. It was an amazing moment. We had pictures taken, but I never hung any up in our house.
>
> About a year after my son got sick, I found the pictures. I wanted to put them up and was looking for a frame. I found a frame that I got when we were first married. It was a beautiful glass picture frame. I had only had it for about six months when it got broken. It had a chip about the size of a quarter in the upper left side. I was very disappointed. We moved several times since I got that frame. I never threw it away. I would always look at it and think what a shame it was that it had that big chip in it. When my son got sick, I just didn't care anymore. I got out the frame and ran my fingers over the chip. I put the picture of my husband and I being blessed by the Pope in it and put it on the table behind my couch.
>
> One day my son was lying on the couch kicking his legs in the air. I was afraid that he would knock over the picture frame so I put the picture face down on the table. I left it like that for the weekend. On Monday, as I was cleaning, I put

the picture back in an upright position. The chip was totally gone. The frame that was chipped for 6 years had healed itself. Now, whenever I have doubts as to whether or not my son will get better, I look to that frame for my strength. I got my sign. I don't know how my story will end. His doctors tell me that with his type of encephalitis, kids will spontaneously come out of it between 22 and 26 months. We are not there yet. But I would put all my bets on the fact that he will recover.

Similarly, Julia, mother to Adam, told me of an occasion when Adam was in his bedroom, alone, having just been put down for his afternoon nap. She related, "I heard him in his room and thought I would leave him in there for awhile, about an hour or so. He wasn't unhappy just chatty and giggly. When I went up to get him, there was a basket (that is kept on a table way away from the crib) in the middle of the floor, and all of the stuff was out of it, also in the middle of the floor, and my son was still in his crib!" Furthermore, Julia told me:

I have to share with you something that happened to my family this evening. Me, my husband Adam, and my mother-in-law were downstairs. Over the baby monitor, I heard one of Adam's wind-up music figurines playing. (We have them for decoration; we don't usually wind them up because they are out of reach and we don't want him to break them.) All of us in the room heard it, and my husband went upstairs to get it. When he touched it, it stopped. But it was playing the music like it had just been wound up (fast). When my husband touched it, it stopped and he picked it up and brought it downstairs. We all inspected it over and over and could not figure out how it had been playing on its own. To get it to play again, my husband had to literally wind it up all the way—which, to me, would mean that when it was playing the first time it had been wound up all the way. It's not defective.

What I found interesting about this is that we were all just discussing my husband's grandfather (who has passed a long time ago). This is the same person with whom Adam has a connection. The musical figurine is of two cows dressed like angels (Mary's Moo Moos—I used to collect them), and the song it was playing was "Angels We Have *Herd* on High." I thought I would share this with you. I was so happy that someone other than me witnessed this as well. Even my husband, who usually can debunk anything, was stumped (he's still trying to figure it out). To me, it's just another validation of what we already know.

And, finally, from Washington State, comes another exceptional and puzzling anecdote:

My mother is a teacher of "developmentally delayed" (perhaps we need to find yet a better phrase) grade school students, and has several very autistic students. My mom described an incident on a field trip where her student, who was assigned a para-educator to watch only him, disappeared from her care and was found a very short time later by the police about a mile-and-a-half away. No one could figure out how he could have gotten there that fast. Then I heard shortly after that of another autistic child who would disappear so fast when mom's back was turned and would be found at any place he really liked or wanted to be. This child, presuming his intellect, knows when mom's not looking, so she can't see him disappear.

When the person submitting this used the word *disappear*, they literally meant *disappear*, for they were writing to enquire if I had ever heard of anyone with autism bilocating. The term *bilocation* describes the ability for a person, or an object, to appear present in two distinct environs simultaneously. It was a term with which I was unfamiliar, and about dismissed altogether, thinking it would really rile conservative readers, until I looked it up. Low and behold, bilocation has legitimate historical and philosophical roots that correlate to shamanism, paganism, folklore, Hinduism, Buddhism, spiritualism, as well as Jewish *and* Christian mysticism. In fact, a litany of Christian saints and monks are reported to have been adept at experiencing bilocation, resulting from prayer, meditation, and compassion. (For example, in 1774, while preparing for Mass, St. Alphonsus Liguori purportedly entered into a trancelike state and attended to the expiring Pope Clement XIV in his cell. His presence

at the Pope's bedside was confirmed by witnesses though he appeared
not to have left his original location—four travel-days away!) According
to one source, "In Christianity, bilocation explains the dual location of
Christ at the Last Supper in both the transubstantiated host and in the
person of Jesus of Nazareth. This idea was important in Catholicism,
which acknowledged that Christ was fully present in the Eucharist."

When I thought about it, I *had* read about the concept of bilocation only it was called an out-of-body-experience or *astral projection*,
whereby the physical body, in a meditative trance (or sleep state) willfully, or subconsciously, projects a *double* in an alternative environment,
which may appear to be a solid duplicate of the actual person, or may
appear translucent or "ghostly." Accounts of ordinary people who have
endured unusual journeys out-of-body are covered in numerous books.
For the layperson, though, I'll admit this is pretty wild. Complicating
matters, I came to understand that, while my contact was referring to
bilocation—being present in two locations at once—she was really asking about *relocation* and reappearance in another place. Now, as many
parents of young children with autism can attest, this is nothing new, so
much so that their son or daughter may be the modern-day kin of the
famous escape artist, Houdini. Oftentimes that child can—in a matter of
rapid seconds and just as soon as mom or dad's back is turned—unlock,
unhinge, maneuver, and dismantle any kind of household alarm system, be it makeshift or professionally installed. It is also not uncommon that those same kids have the uncanny ability to reach the focal
point of their driven destination swiftly, silently, and in the blink of an
eye. There's even a term for it: *elopement*. Nothing so odd about that,
I thought, but for the sake of being thorough I decided to research the
theory of relativity and quantum physics on the off-chance that there
really might be something more to it (at the risk of sounding more like
science fiction than science fact).

FINAL FRONTIERS

I must confess I'm an arty-Aspie, not a techy-Aspie, so understanding the foundation of quantum physics was a real stretch for me, even
when poring over books written for pedestrian readers. But, despite my
fumbling with the subject matter, I did find a few passages that sounded

relevant and worthy of contemplation as it pertained to the idea of relocation. In *The Tao of Physics: An Exploration of the Parallels Between Modern Physics and Eastern Mysticism* (Boston, Mass.: Shambhala Publications, Inc.; 1999), author, Fritjof Capra, writes, "In the words of Chuang Tzu: 'My connection with the body and its parts is dissolved. My perceptive organs are discarded. Thus leaving my material form and bidding farewell to my knowledge, I become one with the Great Pervader. This I call sitting and forgetting all things.'" Capra also explains that Eastern mystics associate concepts of space and time to certain states of consciousness, "Being able to go beyond the ordinary state through meditation, they have realized that the conventional motions of space and time resulting from their mystical experiences appear to be in many ways similar to the notions of modern physics, as exemplified by the theory of relativity. [Which is] based on the discovery that all space and time measurements are relative."

Capra next provides a diagram illustration for the relativity of perception (being very visual, this aided my comprehension immeasurably): two men, one on the left and one on the right, both perceive an umbrella positioned above and between them; but left, right, up, and down depends entirely upon who's doing the observing, and is, thus, relative (which also echoes Wally's admonitions about memory and perception). Contentions made are that the laws of physics are the same for all observers in uniform motion relative to one another, and, as per relativity of simultaneity, "two events, simultaneous for one observer, may not be simultaneous for another observer if the observers are in relative motion." In reverse, this is why I slammed on the brakes—though my car was already in park—the first time I tried a new car wash in which my vehicle remained stationary while the equipment moved around it. The sensation of movement was an illusion as I sat still but *felt* like my car was moving, though to an outside observer the car plainly remained at a standstill. (This concept is also used advantageously in certain amusement park attractions.)

So basically when it comes to simultaneously observed occurrences, my reality is my reality based upon my relative position and individual perceptions. For example, my perception of a vacuum cleaner is that of a machine designed for a specific task; my dog's perception is that the vacuum is alive and roaring ferociously, a threat to her territory; and, to someone vibrating at a higher frequency, the vacuum cleaner is not only the sum of particular parts (a motor, a rotating brush, and so on), it also carries with it the energy from the sources that contributed to the creation of those parts in addition to the energy from the person(s) who assembled it. My perceptions are different from your perceptions, which are different from my dog's perceptions, which are different from the very young child with autism's perceptions, who is unaware of—could give a hoot about—my jaded, adult perceptions of reality and what is and is not possible within the parameters of that framework. He only knows that he wants what he wants and will attain it by whatever means he can! Does this require employing magician-like tactics natural to him, but unnatural to those of us who are shunted from understanding, remembering, and recalling the magic trick by rote?

Max Planck, German physicist and founder of the quantum theory, is considered to be one of the most important physicists of the 20th century. In his study of the energy of light quantum, Planck discovered that such energy increases with frequency—the higher the frequency, the higher the energy; the lower the frequency, the lower the energy. As Gary Zukav explains in *The Dancing Wu Li Masters: An Overview of the New Physics* (William Morrow, 1979), "Energy is proportional to frequency, and Planck's constant is the 'constant of proportionality' between them. This simple relation between frequency and energy is important. It is central to quantum mechanics....When we put wave mechanics and Planck's discovery together we get this: High-frequency light, such as violet light, has a short wavelength and high energy; low-frequency light, such as red light, has a long wavelength and low energy.... This explains the photoelectric effect. Photons of violet light knock electrons loose from the atoms of a metal and send them flying away at a higher velocity than photons of red light, because the photons of violet light, which is a high-frequency light, have more energy than the photons of red light, which is a low-frequency light."

I have long contended, where wavelengths and energy and vibrating molecules are concerned, that many people with autism naturally buzz and vibrate at a much higher frequency than the average person as it relates to perceiving with all the senses, and beyond. (Most particularly, this may apply to those autistics that experience synaesthesia, a kaleidoscopic, crossed-wires ability to "taste" color and "smell" music.)

Does this translate to some children and adults with autism holding the ability to, in essence, convey, "Beam me up, Scotty" in order to teleport to remote locations at will? I don't know; though I do recollect that a presenter at a children's spirituality conference I attended told of similar principles uncovered when interviewing a young girl—the child had told the presenter that she almost passed through a wall but, upon penetrating the physical barrier halfway, she became scared and bumped her head backing out. While I may be rather doubtful, I've since learned never to say never.

By theological standards, I am reminded of an unusual vision I once had. In the middle of the night, I awoke from a dream in which I was walking about a downtown area of a small village with another man. I looked up at a sculpture of the Virgin Mary on a church to see that she had tear-stains of dried blood on her face. In that moment—and very vividly—I smelled roses and I began to levitate in sheer ecstasy. A while afterward I had a similar dream in which I achieved the same effect when contemplating my adoration for Jesus Christ. Memories of both dreams remain realistic sensations. (Incidentally, levitation of objects using laboratory physics *has* been scientifically reproduced, but I'm speaking here of the purity of emotional bliss.)

The word *levitation* is derivative of the Latin word for *lightness*, and Christian history is sprinkled with accounts of holy personages that purportedly attained a physically elevating lightness through altered states of consciousness (hence the idea for *The Flying Nun* television series). While levitating, even in a dream state, may seem fairly spectacular I must stress that, in my case, it was not at all remarkable; it was *secondary*— a naturally-occurring byproduct—to the religious ecstasy I experienced. Perhaps this is the key for understanding the capacity some of us hold, which seems impossible or totally foreign to others.

My beloved friend, Michael, sheds light on how all of this chapter's content fits with the big picture in terms of extraordinary possibilities that begin with an appreciation of autistic functioning:

> We are one soul. To understand that as our origin, dictates an atmosphere of love. To love others as self is the ultimate goal for all of us. Imagine if you physically felt all others' pain; it is the experience of the soul. Treating others as

you would wish to be treated may seem a simple concept, but it escapes practice. How does it relate to autism? Now you've come to my accounting.

We as autists start out in life with meaningless interactions. It is our senses which provide our understanding, give meaning to the world. Autism is based in sensory dysfunction, senses reading too much, too little, or inaccurately [shades of the Intense World Syndrome]. This is as true of me, as the low-functioning autist whose senses did not work at all, as well as the Asperger's individual who fails to process the subtlest of cues. The senses are like light with so many wavelengths invisible to the naked eye. To understand me as an extreme may help differentiate at least some of the possibilities.

According to *Star Trek* space is man's final frontier but, if this is so, I believe it pertains to both outer and *inner* space. Modern-day medical science continues to evolve in ways that are increasingly sophisticated and accurate, and we've only just scratched the surface in understanding the psychology of mental wellness—diagnoses of which are, essentially, educated guesswork. Pioneering the frontier of inner space by plotting the constellations of its celestial mentality is something humankind has yet to fully address in a manner that is comprehensive and accessible to all. The realm of the human mind is intangible, indistinguishable from the human brain, and yet it exists in depths and fathoms unrealized. What are the borders of its potential and how do we measure miracles if extraordinary feats of pure thought become *ordinary*? Perhaps one day the power of the mind will be charted in accordance with medical science or even space exploration. I suspect, then, that the adage about imagination knowing no bounds will seem elementary in its naïveté.

Chapter 4

Knowledge Is Power

*"Every great advance in natural knowledge has involved
the absolute rejection of authority."*
—Thomas Henry Huxley

Many parents, professionals, and, particularly, readers of my work, know of the painful, acute, and exquisite sensory sensitivities experienced by their loved one with autism. Sensory sensitivities are hyper-reactions, or overstimulation, to abrupt, spontaneous, and assaultive environmental stimuli. For the uninitiated, examples may include the following:

✴ *Vision*: Many people on the autism spectrum (but not all) take in everything they see and filter out nothing. They tend to be detail people. Many are visual thinkers and learners; cognitive thought occurs in visual streams of pictures and movies, and they can recall and replay these images in minutiae—this includes positive, loving experiences as well as those traumatic. Visual stressors can take the form of certain colors or an extreme sensitivity to lighting, particularly artificial lighting (fluorescent and halogen), but even intense sunlight. Exposure to such may be physically exhausting and draining. This can affect vision, causing it to be blurred; it can distort depth perception and a person's ability to move and ambulate.

✴ *Auditory*: Unpredictable noises such as loud voices, coughing, laughing, sneezing; dogs barking; sirens and fire alarms;

babies or other children screaming or crying; vacuum cleaners; lights and fans humming may be startling and assaultive. They cannot usually be *predicted*.

* *Smells and Tastes*: Certain individuals with autism may gag or vomit at just the sight or smell of certain foods. Some children's palates are so sensitive that some foods and food textures are intolerable, ranging from soft or slimy foods (Jell-O, pudding) to crunchy textures (celery, carrots). Resistance to foods may also be associated with memories (forced feeding of food, or painful textures in the mouth and throat). Food allergies to dyes, preservatives, casein (dairy), and gluten (wheat and other grains) can manifest itself in conduct linked to digestive problems.

* *Touch*: Skin can be exquisitely sensitive, and some autistics might be limited in the types of fabric that their skin can tolerate, such as cotton. Clothes that feel fine to the average person might need to be washed repeatedly to soften them; tags might need to be cut out. Sometimes used clothing is preferable, since it has a long history of being worn. (Certain individuals may also be hypo-sensitive, or under-sensitive, *and* still have acute hyper-sensitivities.) Deep-pressure sensation, such as swaddling in a comforter, blanket, or sleeping bag, is a way to decompress and reorganize before re-entering the sensory-insensitive world.

It is these supersonic sensitivities that predispose those most susceptible among us, including autistics, to perceive all things seen and unseen; that is, information filtered out or disregarded by others. As you've learned, in addition to environmental reactions, this may also manifest in correlation to heightened-frequency stimuli as related to all the senses in a manner some would call *spiritual*.

It is also characteristic of most individuals on the autism spectrum to be *very literal* in their interpretation of what they perceive. Deliberate deception occurs infrequently and is usually transparent (meaning, we're ineffective liars even when we try). Imaginative play, though deemed clinically absent in autism, usually occurs in tandem with those activities for which the individual is most passionate, such as when playing with Thomas the Tank, Barbie, or horse or marine-life figurines, for example. Given these caveats, it is advised that parents, professionals, and caregivers should receive unconventional information of a spiritual nature observed or shared with them as the individual's *truth* regardless of personal perceptions (remember it's all relative). Given the rising frequency of such unusual happenings (making them more and more *usual*), I have devised a spiritual protocol to which families may adhere and refer. Further, concerned caregivers are advised to:

✳ Honor and acknowledge the individual's experiences as her truth.

✳ Maintain ethics of disclosure (and do not do so without the individual's permission).

✳ Refrain from sensationalizing the individual's experiences, making them more dramatic than they are.

✳ Take respectful measures to support the individual to feel safe and comfortable.

A SPIRITUAL PROTOCOL

It is important for caregivers to maintain a healthy skepticism as well as bear an open mind in investigating the information observed or shared by the individual with autism. Not everything is *something*. Please don't get carried away to extremes; some experiences have perfectly logical explanations. The individual who thinks in pictures and movies, and appears to be talking to someone unseen, may be verbally *replaying* an authentic or fictional event, such as role-playing a favorite cartoon scene or a particularly delightful time with an indulgent grandpa or aunt. Use this knowledge to temper perceptions; however, this example may be considered the exception to the rule.

Through my research, which includes more than 20 years of experience supporting, interviewing, and corresponding with individuals with autism and their caregivers, I have determined that one of the most common spiritual experiences for individuals on the autism spectrum (especially infants and toddlers) is a perceived interaction with the essence or presence of a deceased grandparent. These events may transpire through:

✳   A playful interaction with someone unseen (though a presence may be sensed by a caregiver) in which the individual
with autism laughs, chortles, or giggles; plays peek-a-boo-
type activities; appears to be tickled; or points or gazes to a
specific area of the room.

✳   Similar activity occurring during the night *but* the individual is well-rested the following day, with no symptoms of
sleeplessness.

✳   Verbal reports, from the individual with autism, of seeing
grandma or grandpa.

✳   The ability to identify grandma or grandpa from family photographs, to know details of their lives, and to know their first
names—despite no one having ever shared this information—
regardless of whether grandparent and grandchild *ever met.*

Here is an example of one such occurrence from Petra in Germany:

When I was around 6 years old, my grandmother (mother
of my father) was very ill. I didn't know how much, but she
was bedridden for a couple of months when, one day, all
the brothers and sisters from my father came to our house.
Our family was the only one who lived in the same town
like my grandma, so it was no wonder they came all to us.
I knew that something special would be happening, but no
one told me what. The children of my grandma went to
her, the other relatives stood with my mother, my brother,
and me at our home. And we waited. Everyone tried to
be silent. Everything was so strange to me. I took my most
loved book and crawled under my bed.

Only a short time later I knew what had happened—my
grandma had died. I think only a minute after that thought
the telephone rings. And only another minute later my one
cousin came into my room and told me that my thought
has come true. Curiously I wasn't able to be sad like all the
others. I only felt a big silence inside.

A few days later—before the funeral—my parents
wanted to go to an evening service. It was not the first

time but the times before, one of my grandmothers always babysit at my brother and me. But this time we should stay at home alone. My parents went to church and my brother and I laid in our beds (we had a bunk bed and I laid at the top). Then my grandma was in our room. I think my brother slept, but I was awake. She read something from my book and brought me some sweets. And then she told me that this was the last time she could be with me. I said that I know it and everything was fine. At the next moment, I heard my parents and turned my head to the door. That was the moment my grandma left me. I told my father what happened and he said that that was something very special and I should be glad about it and never forget it. That was the first time I got "in contact."

These types of experiences should not be causing distress or upset for the individual (unless someone else is overreacting to the events, causing emotional distress and upset to occur). Unless things progress to the contrary—which I've never heard of—the preceding interactions should be considered comforting, harmless, loving, and positive, as was Petra's case.

Another common experience that shares similarities with the foregoing events, and should also be considered benign, is that in which an individual with autism appears to hold a two-way interaction or conversation with an unseen presence that some have defined as *angelic*. As I've previously documented, this may be interpreted as counseling or mentoring time (after all, being autistic can be an extremely difficult life without guidance from a Higher Power), and should not be extinguished as "behavioral." This experience may transpire through:

✳ An interaction experienced by the individual with autism that usually occurs in solitude at the same place and time with regularity (often daily).

✳ An apparent two-way communion in which the individual with autism attends in rapt command and nods or verbally responds to an unseen presence, as if answering questions or communicating an understanding.

* Any interruptions by a caregiver are respectfully ignored or excluded by the individual from the process, after which the interaction resumes until complete.

* A jubilant emergence from the completed interaction in which the individual is replenished and refreshed, and joyfully seeks to share this sensation with others—even if it is uncharacteristic to do so—through physical touch and intimate interaction.

One instance exemplary of the above comes from Jeannie, mom to Zach:

> I believe my 5-year-old son, Zach, sees and communicates with spirits. I have noticed this behavior since he was 2 years old. He often looks a bit above himself and jibber-jabbers as if he's talking to someone, or they are talking to him. He becomes very animated and it's apparent he is conversing (in his mind) with someone or many. He is now only at the point where he says words not sentences.
>
> Yesterday we had to put our dog, Maxie, down and Zach was at preschool when it happened. When I went back to the veterinarian's office to pay them, after I picked Zach up from school, he became very happy and excited in the lobby of the office. The receptionist even noticed this. Then he pointed to my eyes and said "eyes." Then he turned my face to look over my shoulder at something that wasn't there. At first I didn't pick up on it, until we got in the car. I again saw him in the back seat appear to be looking, smiling, and communicating with someone beside him who I could not see. I suspected he was talking to someone who was holding Maxie. I said to him, "Maxie died and went to Heaven today," and he smiled and looked at me and said "Sun." This is a really big deal to me because, like I said, he doesn't communicate that well and for him to say the word *sun* in response to Heaven is very telling I think, especially since I haven't specifically talked with him about Heaven that I remember.

Similar experiences may also be sensed by other family members who are present as witnesses. Remember: a loving presence will only ever be a loving presence, and will never cause distress, fear, anxiety, upset, or intrusions of any kind. Their way is simple, subtle, and altogether awesome, like the increasingly familiar phenomena visible in pictures only after the fact.

SPHERES OF ENERGY

Tangible evidence of a loving, spiritual presence may manifest through digital photography in which unexplainable white starbursts or streaks of white light appear, or perfectly symmetrical spheres of energy, commonly called orbs, are evident. The orbs may appear as whitish, circular blobs that are nearly see-through (most people, unaware, completely overlook them as photographic blips or anomalies). In rare cases, orbs may be colored brilliant blues or purples, or soft pinks. Their size may vary from very small to very large, and sometimes more than one can manifest in a photograph. They are noticed with increasing frequency in keeping with widespread use of digital photography, which captures imagery at a greater speed than previously obtained through standard cameras.

Now, not everything is something, and oftentimes photographic orbs can be explained as light refractions of dust specks or moisture in the air. For example, I have seen photographs taken outdoors on, say, misty evenings at dusk, and the atmosphere is literally filled with dozens of orbs, of all sizes, scattered about. In my opinion, this is a naturally-occurring phenomenon with a rational explanation—light from the camera reflecting off of fine mist.

On the other hand, I have seen some pretty spectacular photographs shared with me by humble families who seek nothing more than validation from someone who understands. In one instance, a family, whom I had met in person, forwarded to me two photos of interest taken a second or two apart. In the first, a male relative (an uncle, I think) is interacting with a young boy with autism (their son) who is seated in his high-chair. In the background of this picture is a translucent orb about the size of a basketball when compared in proportion to the setting. This, alone, is fairly noteworthy, but in the *next consecutive photograph,* taken but a moment later, the same orb has *moved*, maintaining its shape and size, to relocate in the foreground of the environment. And that, my friends, ain't no dust speck! Sometimes careful observers who enlarge orb photos on a computer screen can make out "faces" or other images contained within the orbs. I have yet to discern a face in an orb blow-up that actually *looks like a face* to me, but I have seen interesting patterns including what resembled a gorgeous rose in bloom—with scalloped edges and distinct layers of flower petals—in a wedding picture of a groom dancing with his bride.

The source of authentic orb occurrences is open to postulation. Some believe them to be indicators for the presence of a loved one who has crossed over, a grandparent for instance. Such has been the interpretation of my young comrade, Christopher. The morning after we met for our first consultation, I was preparing for a presentation at a local church when he asked if his mother could take a snapshot of the two of us together. Posed side by side, with our arms around one another, I felt paternal warmth for this young man with Asperger's as we bonded in the moment. But upon examining the picture afterward, I am actually flanked by two presences—Christopher on my right and a grapefruit-sized orb on my left that resembles a silvery ball of yarn suspended in mid-air. Subsequent photos of us on a follow-up occasion reveal additional orbs that Christopher took as an indication for the presence of his great-grandmother, who had passed away only weeks prior. (Indeed, families may be more likely to note orbs in pictures taken on special occasions when relatives are united and loving emotions are running strong and high, such as the birth of a baby, or a birthday, anniversary, or holiday celebration.)

Others believe that orbs represent a protective spiritual presence such as an angel or an emissary from God. In my opinion it makes no difference, and the source may be delineated in keeping with personal interpretations that provide comfort or consolation. Again, and as before, so long as these experiences are not creating anxiety and fear for the individual with autism there is no further intervention required, and encounters with purported high-vibration presences, such as angels, should be received as a unique blessing.

The morning of November 6, 2008: Christopher, the author, and an orb. (Photo courtesy D. Cully).

Chapter 5

Spiritual Warfare

As I was going up the stair
I saw a man who wasn't there
He wasn't there again today
I wish, I wish he'd stay away.
—William Hughes Mearns

A late-2008 posting to a parents-of-kids-with-autism Internet message board was beginning to sound almost as perseverative as the repetitious video-snippet repeatedly rewound by the average autistic child:

> Taylor always was a good sleeper. He still is. However for the past week he will scream (and I mean SCREAM!) when I go downstairs at night. Usually we ignore him and let him scream, but, man, is it annoying! I think it is an attention thing. What would you do? He is not in pain or trying to hurt himself.

An "attention thing" would be a typically expedient way to deduce Taylor's bedtime conduct (indeed, as many parents can attest, screaming at night when one should be sleeping definitely gets *attention*). But is it that facile? A child deigned *always a good sleeper* is only just now screaming (*loudly*) after being tucked in, upstairs alone in bed—every night for the past week. And he doesn't appear to be in pain nor is he self-injurious, both of which might be indications of physical or emotional distress. I had to wonder: is there something more to Taylor's terrified outbursts than what meets the eye?

The Internet posting was but one of a rash of similar online vents I began to observe at a time when such reports were coinciding with my own observations of something potentially sinister afoot. Where there is good, there is evil. As much as many people with autism are of a high-vibration frequency—open to accessing many astounding acts of spiritual giftedness—those same persons are also wide open to receiving the influence of very negative energies generated by the malcontent of other people near to them, or by presences unseen and unknown. (Eventually the negativity of both parties conjoins, as you will read.) Through my books and research I have accounted for what I believe to be significant encounters of many autistics with presences of ill-intent—circumstances for which physical pain, issues of mental wellness, and "attention-seeking behavior" have all been ruled out. In those cases, the impetus manifesting such exasperating nocturnal escapades was something more... something seemingly predatory. Allow me to explain.

As much as I believe in the existence of God, Heaven, angels, and souls of the dearly departed, I also think that there are harmful, bodiless entities that roam the universe seeking prey in the form of unsuspecting victims who, in physical form, serve as hosts to which these entities may attach just like a magnet. If you, too, can believe this is possible, I offer several explanations for why they may do this:

* They're evil or incorrigible at best.
* They fear a wrathful or vengeful God who will punish them so they avoid the Heavenly realm.
* They hold no esteem for self-worth and feel that God will reject them if they near Him.
* They've been away from God for so long they forget that they, too, originated in His Divine Presence.
* They're lonely and attaching to someone physical mimics feeling human once more.
* They're bent on causing destruction in order to fulfill a mission of chaos.

Based on the preceding list, it may sound as if such presences could be defined as either *ghosts* or *demons*. In fact, there have been occasions when I, myself, have been uncertain. In my opinion and in my experience, ghosts are earth-bound human souls that either don't realize they're dead or they resist leaving the physical world for being so self-absorbed. In the latter instance, it is usually a low-energy, negative emotion that restrains them here such as depression, addiction, abuse, rage, jealousy, revenge, and so on. They ignore (or deliberately decline to see) the Heavenly realm; instead, they exist in a gray, vapid void with their backs turned away from Heaven which, if they could see it, would appear as a tiny pinpoint of light. If they had the sense to approach the pinpoint of light, it would grow in brightness and glow with intensity the closer they gained toward it until they are home at last in an atmosphere of tranquility and unconditional love. (Thus, I have never found it cute or funny whenever anyone tells me they have a "friendly ghost" at home. That's not okay—they're not supposed to be there!) On the other hand, I am uncertain if demons have ever been human (they are fallen angels, by some). They seem to be more powerful and aggressive than ghosts, and capable of greater harm though, they, too, originated in God, the Source of all Creation; they just refuse to acknowledge it.

Perfect Victims

The individual with autism makes for the perfect victim in cases of negative spirit attachment for a number of reasons. It is the extreme perceptive capabilities and extraordinary sensitivity that attracts negative presences to the random person with autism. If that person is being so plagued *and* doesn't speak, he or she is also likely to be labeled as intellectually inferior (mentally retarded). Under such conditions, the individual doesn't have a way to communicate their terror other than by what gets interpreted as behavioral outbursts, *and* no one would know the difference because the majority of parents and caregivers have been led to believe that extreme behaviors are conducive to being autistic! Even if the individual speaks, it doesn't mean they know how to use language to describe what they're experiencing, or otherwise express it in a manner that won't be belittled or dismissed as nonsense. This feeds a vicious cycle in which unusual circumstances that *are* reported are then treated as hallucinatory and subsequently treated with psychopharmacology (sedating drugs). Keeping someone down and enmeshed in a vicious cycle is *precisely* what ill-intended entities *want*. It keeps the host from reviving and gives the entities the low-energy nourishment that sustains them—they thrive on chaos and fear. (If they fed from higher-vibration emotions, like joy, they wouldn't be here.)

Recently, I spoke about this very predicament as a potential reality to about 75 interested parents of children with autism. Even though I was clear in communicating cautions about jumping to conclusions, a number of them felt that such circumstances were unequivocally the case for their own child. I found it necessary to remind them: not everything is something. If a person with autism is communicating through extreme measures, parents and caregivers must first exercise sound judgment by exploring the following:

* Physical pain and discomfort that is undetected, undiagnosed, untreated, and has become chronic, which is giving rise to outrageous conduct in efforts to convey the pain via an autistic version of charades.

* Respect within the relationship in conjunction with a presumption of intellect—is this being communicated, and, if not, have apologies been made by seeking forgiveness from the person with autism?

* Overwhelming reactions to environmental sensory stimuli that conspires to bombard and overload the individual, impairing his or her ability to function.

* Overwhelming emotional reactions to events of which others believe the individual is unaware or unconcerned about but which, in reality, are weighing heavily upon him or her and causing tremendous distress.

* Legitimate issues of mental wellness most common of which are acute anxiety (due to not having control over knowing what's to expect and what's expected, or not being informed about what's coming next), depression, bipolar disorder, and post-traumatic stress disorder.

Further, once these measures have been thoroughly exhausted, parents must examine the household atmosphere and the general tone of the family environment. Oftentimes there is friction, tension, and great stress within the family (*not* directly involving the individual) such as marital discord, alcoholism or substance abuse, and depression.

DISCERNING ILL INTENT

What follows is the litmus-test protocol I have developed after interviewing, observing, and consulting with countless families undergoing something deeply upsetting, and for which they have no explanation. It may all seem unbelievable but, rest assured, it is very real and happening to many families. Experiences of ill intent may transpire through the following symptoms:

✳ The individual with autism experiences regular, if not nightly, night terrors or grotesque nightmares (beyond just an occasional bad dream), which may be accompanied by bedwetting.

✳ The individual habitually awakens between midnight and 3 a.m. feeling absolutely terrified, oftentimes screaming, crying, or yelling.

✳ The individual becomes increasingly anxious, or procrastinates, as bedtime approaches, with complaints about sleeping in his or her own bedroom.

✳ The individual is unwilling to sleep alone and is only comforted by falling asleep elsewhere (prior to a caregiver transferring them to their own bed), or sleeping with family members.

✳ For those who speak, the individual reports black figure-shaped shadows, hooded figures, ghostly figures, or monstrous "demonic" entities with red eyes that threaten harm, or give harmful instructions (such as inciting self-injury or injury against others).

✳ The individual displays acute hyperactivity and anxiety during the daytime, or an intense increase in reckless or self-injurious conduct which, if allowed to become chronic, may result in a legitimate mental health diagnosis. Parents experiencing such episodes are often prescribed Risperdal for their children.

✳ The perpetuation of negative emotions and events in the individual's environment(s) such as depression, hopelessness, fear, revenge, envy, rage, avarice, addiction, and abuse.

✳   Unseen physical manipulation or interference of electricity
     in the household, such as devices scrambling, malfunction-
     ing, or operating independently (this includes TVs, radios,
     computers, and telephones).

✳   Household objects (a hairbrush or toy) or small, portable
     electronic devices (a cell phone) go missing from where they
     had last been seen and may manifest in a totally unrelated
     place.

✳   Family pets, particularly dogs, may seem increasingly anx-
     ious, "clingy," and in need of constant attention or reassur-
     ances. (I meet *a lot* of very nervous dogs that will not leave
     me alone, want to "tell" me something, and only relax once
     I explain the truth.)

As many parents know all too well, sleep disturbances are com-
monplace in persons with autism, and preventative measures should be
taken to assess if an individual's sleep quality is affected by medication
side-effects, allergic reactions (including food), or anxiety over not having enough control or independence. The difference here pertains to an
individual's abject fear, if not terror, upon awakening during the night
and that this occurs on a *frequent* basis.

DEVIL IN THE DETAILS

I encourage my readers to remain critical yet open-minded in learning about spiritual assaults such as what I've just described. A good
example of how not everything is something occurred when an agency
staff person took me to visit Margaret and her two children Toby and
Ellie, both on the autism spectrum, who lived in a trailer on the edge of
a forested area.

Using my own heightened sensitivity, I intuited that an alcoholic
male had previously resided in the trailer. Margaret confirmed this, and
told me he had died while *en flagrante* (the woman he was with had
sprinted into the night half-dressed). Both children had been grappling
with sleep issues, especially since their father left a couple years before.
Toby, in particular, had been having nightmares, wetting the bed, and
demonstrating spikes of aggression. He was heavily interested in *Star*

Wars and when I asked him the eye color of the creatures in his dreams, he said they always have something red around or over their eyes.

As the electricity, phone, and dog were all fine (the dog greeted me, rolled over so I could rub her belly, then took off to do her own thing), I surmised that it's more an issue of unresolved conflict with dad who is a drug addict, deals drugs, misses opportunities to meet with the children, and has had grandiose ideas, such as perceiving every bird he sees to be an eagle or always seeing UFOs. He was also witnessed in the woods outside their trailer from the bathroom window, so the children were afraid of going to the bathroom alone for fear that he was stalking them from the trees. Both children felt lots of hyper-vigilance and anxiety for having been verbally threatened by dad in the past, and they were present when dad shouted that he was going to kill Margaret.

The agency staff person and I crafted a plan for the family to have a consistent evening routine (checking locked windows and doors, reading bedtime stories, and reaffirming their love for one another) to feel safe and comfortable and in control of the environment. We also suggested to Margaret that a window shade or curtain be put up in the bathroom to create a visual block for the children. Regrettably, as dad had only threatened harm but had not yet acted upon it, there was nothing further that could be done legally to protect Margaret and her children. For the time being, I believe the family's experiences to stem from natural consequences. For the time being.

Contrast the preceding situation with another consultation that took place in the *same week* for Jesse, 11 years old, and his family: mom, dad, Bob; brother, Jamie; and sister, Janie, who were all gathered together awaiting my arrival. Without being told anything except Jesse's first name and age (and I am adamant about this stipulation as agency staff with whom I have worked will tell you), and prior to arriving at the family's home, I surmised that the environment was in total chaos and the agency staff person accompanying me affirmed this. Upon entering the house, the family dog, Barkley, would not leave me alone, wanting constant attention, stroking, and comfort. Despite being softly reprimanded and called away, Barkley positioned himself directly in front of me, placed a paw on my lap, and peered deeply into my eyes.

Not wishing to waste any time during the family interview, I asked mom to cut to the chase and tell me honestly about the stress and tension in the house. She said it was mostly financial stress and that she was depressed; there was also stress for Jesse's "behaviors" and Jamie's health issues.

I learned that, for years, Jesse had experienced sleep disturbances. The family had been in the present house 15 years, but, as a baby, Jesse would look up and past mom at the ceiling. Later, he began having night terrors, complaining of monsters under his bed. He was taking Melatonin to induce sleep, but still awakened during the night (before 3 a.m.) and got into bed with his parents, even though he shared a bedroom with his brother.

There'd also been some spill-over events in real-time for other family members. One of Jamie's friends had seen and heard things in the house. Mom said she'd seen something move in the background in the mirror while drying her hair; though she knew she was alone in the house, she still stopped to go and look (no one and nothing was there). And Janie showed me where a bedroom lamp had physically changed location several times upon re-entering her bedroom, jumping from one side of a nightstand to the other. Additionally, light bulbs had flickered or blown, the computer had malfunctioned, and small objects had gone missing only to turn up later (as did an iPod, which reappeared in Jamie's schoolbag that he had previously searched). Lastly, Jesse had become increasingly aggressive, usually toward mom whom he had bitten. He'd also thrown knives out the window and crawled out onto the second floor roof with a knife. He had screamed and cursed at Jesus Christ, the family told me.

I discussed the protocol for determining ill intent; the need to re-envision Jesse's behavior as communication attempts and reactions; and the importance of creating predictable structure for Jesse by implementing a picture schedule of daily routines for him to follow along.

I next walked the house with the family, feeling especially uncomfortable about an ancient-looking floor grate (that led to the basement); a bathroom (next to the basement entrance, and where lights had flickered); and, of course, the basement itself. (A new family room addition felt void and clear to me.) Upon descending into it, the basement felt "heavy." I had previously picked up a male and female presence, and felt the male in the basement, especially near a far corner. Bob said he worked down in the basement and had felt uncomfortable, and Jamie reported that Jesse had seen someone down there as well. I asked if Jesse had reported seeing any unusual eye color and he mentioned red eyes, and focused on glowing eyes.

Coming upstairs, I sensed that I was intended to see a bedroom. (Climbing the stairs to the second floor, I "felt" the small woman running quickly up and down them so I asked if anyone ever felt a cold spot there; mom said she had, but thought it might've just been from the window there, which it could have been.)

I was shown Jamie and Jesse's room, a typical boys' room in disarray, but it clearly wasn't the bedroom I felt compelled to see. I asked about the master bedroom, and, once there, my stomach dropped with queasiness and I went weak in the knees. I was firm in stating that the master bedroom was the seat of a lot of stress and tension in the home, and mom said it was where bills were paid online and finances argued about. (The agency staff person later told me that Jesse said he had seen the man I had sensed seated on the bed in that room.) Next, Janie showed me her bedroom with the small candlestick lamp that moved from one side of a small end table to another. She also said she had heard "music-box music" outside her bedroom.

Next was the attic where I, again, felt the woman's presence. I asked if any of the neighbors had ever reported seeing the light on there, and indeed, they *had*, although the family couldn't be sure if it was because a light had been left on. I also felt that the woman solemnly looked out an attic window, and the agency staff person later told me she heard a woman say "Help." Jamie said his friend heard and saw a woman up there, too.

Later, in the family room, Jesse was pretend "smoking" with his lollipop stick and I felt he was emulating someone. I asked the family if any of them ever caught a fleeting whiff of tobacco and they said not, but I remained firm in reiterating that the male presence smoked. Afterward, this was affirmed by the agency staff person who said Jesse had reported seeing the man with red eyes smoking outside.

In summary of my visit with Jesse's family, it was evident that I intuited lots of spot-on validations, which I think helped the family to perceive me as credible, and possibly caused dad, Bob (who I think was quite skeptical), to believe in my authenticity.

YEAR OF THE PHANTOM

If such events still strain reason for any reader, I submit, for your consideration and reflection, the following journal entries of similar incidents tallied throughout the course of 12 months. I have included a sampling of only the most significant incidents, but all occurred solely within my home territory and in my work consulting for just *one* agency. If but only a fraction of these incidents are to be believed, what's happening elsewhere in the world?

March 16, 2007

After mentoring my colleague, Brett, through a particularly distressing situation he submitted the following summary of events:

> Evan is a sensitive 5-year-old boy who has undergone a great transformation. Evan has always been very loving and kind to those who spend time with him. He would always run up to staff members and give us a hug when we came to his house to work with him. He enjoyed doing lots of different activities, reading, and just generally being around others. Then, slowly, Evan began to change as factors yet unknown were affecting him.
>
> Evan began to only want to spend time in his room and would become extremely upset when he would be expected to leave his room, even to play or eat. He would scream at anyone who kept him out of his room and not want to interact with anyone. This progressed to the point that Evan would spend all day every day in his room if allowed to. When the support aide came to visit him for two hours a day, it would be a great struggle throughout the session. He would yell, hit, run away, cry, and demand to be left to return to his room. Because of these instances, his mother decided to talk to me about "other problems" that Evan was dealing with. She approached this topic with great trepidation as she

was unsure of what response I would have to what she was about to tell me.

The topics discussed were more spiritual in nature, and the mother's way of describing the incidents were that Evan may be being visited by "a ghost." She described how he was no longer sleeping during the night and that she could hear him talking to someone in his room. Evan was clearly upset by the person he was speaking to because he was not allowed to sleep! His mood continued to deteriorate as he slept less and less. Eating also became more sporadic. Evan's mother asked him about whom he was speaking to. Evan told her that there was an old man in his room talking to him.

At this point, Evan's mother told me that both she and her daughter have also seen an older man in the house throughout the years, not of physical nature. They were both afraid of this person and did not want to be in the house alone, especially at night. They both also stated that they oftentimes felt that someone was behind them when they would go up the stairs to the second floor, even when there was no one nearby. I believe that the mother confided in me because Evan's behavior had progressed to such a point that she was unsure how to continue on. She did not want anyone to think that she or Evan was "crazy" or needed to be hospitalized. When I assured her that I did not think that either of them was crazy, but instead believed that something truly could be happening because of Evan's sensitivities, she seemed relieved.

I discussed with Evan's mother some initial things that the family could try to help alleviate the situation and to see if anything else would need to be done. Suggestions made were the following:

✳ Say a prayer of protection before going to bed with Evan. Having dad do this with him may be even more helpful, as he seems very much like Evan and may understand what he is going through.

✳　Equip Evan with the power to say no! To allow him the ability and knowledge that he can tell the being keeping him awake to leave him alone and to go away. Make it part of the bedtime routine to talk about things he can say if there is a problem.

✳　Make sure Evan can ask for help and feels comfortable talking about these things with his parents. They are to assure him that they believe in what he is telling them.

These steps were all taken. The family did begin saying a prayer of protection and equipping Evan with the words to use when he was awoken in the night or anytime he felt that he needed to say something.

Amazingly, Evan started showing a great transformation when his family began taking these steps with him. He went from a boy being drained to the energetic, loving, and cherub-like boy we all knew. He no longer wanted to stay in his room, but instead would again run to greet anyone who came to the house. Evan even told us all that angels watch over him and his parents while they sleep. He no longer is awakened in the night and is sleeping once again.

On a side note, it is interesting that the family was comfortable with saying a prayer before bedtime. The family does not practice any type of religion and did not talk about spiritual subjects ever before this incident. The professional team has been working with the family for more than two years now. Evan has mentioned that at times he talks to Jesus on his mother's cell phone. He will pretend to dial and ask that Jesus keep everyone safe.

March 24, 2007

From another professional associate comes the next entry concerning two of a family's three children. The oldest son has Asperger's Syndrome and the baby is autistic; the middle child, female, is unaffected:

Thanks for getting back to me so quickly. He still isn't sleeping consistently well. He still has huge black bags under his eyes and will not turn off the light. In one of his dreams, he was screaming because he said this thing was going after the little one (his younger brother). Now the little one is getting up at night and wanting to sleep with mom and dad, or running around at night. The other night they took him (the older one) to the hospital because his leg hurt him so badly. The doctor said he probably slept on it wrong or he was trying to get out of school. He didn't know what happened; it could have been a charley horse.

I'm getting him enrolled in a feeding clinic, because he isn't eating. I just don't know if this thing is gone, or under control? He just isn't talking about it. I suggested that his therapist use art therapy techniques. Any other suggestions or do you think he doesn't feel comfortable? I gave him a tiny petrified wooden cross to put around his neck, and we had it blessed. He wore it for about a week then his mom said that it broke. The chain broke and there was a chunk taken out of the cross. Petrified wood is like stone; if he bit it, wouldn't he have hurt his teeth? I'm worried that the older one isn't talking about it because it scares him or it is going after the younger one now, and he can't tell anyone if it is. The first house that they lived in, when this began, mom felt a very uncomfortable presence and saw a figure at one time. That is when the older one first started talking about this. I am going to see the family on Wednesday. I'm sure that it may not be a good time for you so if you give me some times I can arrange the meeting. Mom has been asking about you, she said she felt like she knew you already. I also bought her your book *Autism and the God Connection*.

April 24, 2007

I got an update on the preceding family for whom I consulted: three children, oldest boy, 9, with Asperger's sees a cloaked figure at the foot of his bed telling him to throw himself out the window, or to stab his family; 2-year-old brother also wakes up screaming, running downstairs at night. Uniting the family through an evening bonding session has helped, and the oldest boy went to church and—independently and without prompting—walked up to a statue of Jesus and kissed His feet. His third rosary has broken though; crosses keep falling off.

June 13, 2007

I am invited to meet Ryland, 12, who has Asperger's and symptoms of depression. Ryland and his similar-aged brother, are being raised by their grandparents in a rural Victorian house that sits adjacent to an 1800s-era graveyard; the two properties blend into one another. The boys' mother is reported to have ADD and bipolar disorder (for which she takes no medication), and is transient in their lives, coming to live with them temporarily after failed relationships. They know their grandparents as mother and father. Grandfather is a truck driver and is often on the road.

The home is in disrepair, and cluttered with boxes of garage sale items. There is no air conditioning, only ceiling fans. The wallpaper of the small living room, in which we gather, may even be original to the era; it has large moisture stains and, in part, covers over a fireplace opening, above which is a mantel. It is a curious juxtaposition to see the vintage wallpaper and a bookshelf filled with Disney and other children's videos and anime action figures. Both boys share the same bedroom.

Ryland is gentle and gracious, honest and forthcoming. He almost immediately opens up to tell me about his anxiety and depression (within the past year he attempted suicide by throwing himself out a second story window). He also shared that when he was 5 years old, he was physically attacked by a headless white shape that picked him up and told him, "Don't speak English!" before putting him back down. He refers to this type of entity as "the pounders" because of the knocking noise they make which heralds their approach. Ryland also shared that he saw a young girl in the cemetery and that he knew she must not be local otherwise he would've recognized her from school.

I feel such overwhelming compassion for Ryland as he speaks; he is reminiscent of me at his age, in demeanor, appearance, and life struggles. Before departing I tell him, "Come here to me," which he does willingly. As he leans forward, I kiss his forehead and tell him, "My kiss will protect you, and no one will dare harm the person who bears its mark." I touch the place where my lip imprint lingers before we leave the house.

Cindy, my agency point person, visits the family again the next day, June 14, and is led by grandmother to the kitchen. The night of our visit, the kitchen ceiling fan exploded: two light bulbs shattered across the kitchen floor and the fan blades sheared off, hitting the walls, and were thrown to different parts of the kitchen. Grandmother tells Cindy, "I've never seen anything like this." Cindy and I both conclude that something or someone was unsettled by our presence and by our desire to serve Ryland in ways that would illuminate his gifts and talents, thus bolstering his self-esteem.

The evening of June 14, I receive a lovely and pensive e-mail from Ryland telling me, "I believe in you, I'm not going to stop believing you." He goes on to describe his sensory sensitivities including that he sees "things every day because I see lines in the air that are shaped like people." When this occurs, he doesn't feel secure, and thinks, "Oh crap, something is here that isn't supposed to be."

The night of Cindy's visit, Ryland is awakened in the night by a frightening presence that enters his room and gets into bed with him. Terrified, he goes to his grandmother's bedroom, but cannot rouse her.

Cindy and I hold regular counseling sessions by phone during which we discuss in detail the nature of the situation and how to combat the presences. For now, this includes incorporating family affirmation-time and prayer into Ryland's everyday schedule. At my encouragement, he has also applied to be a speaker at trainings for mental health workers preparing to serve children his age. Cindy also tells me that grandmother has shown Ryland's support aide photographs taken last Christmas that reportedly show white glares.

For more than a week, which included a trip to New York, I feel plagued with consistent and negative misfortune—highly unusual for someone accustomed to good luck. I get into an argument, a tree in my front yard is uprooted in a storm and must be destroyed, I step on my dog and sprain her leg for several days—these in addition to many small irritations, including lots of negative, self-destructive thoughts.

On June 24, I sought the advisement of a group of individuals with autism who do not speak but, instead, type. They suggest that the family move, which I don't think is an option. One man tells me that a statue of St. Christopher is needed for Ryland to have something tangible to hold when he feels frightened; he says that St. Christopher is the boy's guardian. Another person suggested that Ryland should evoke his guardian angel. A female friend with autism typed that Ryland needs a circle. When I asked for clarification, thinking she meant a "circle of support," human-services lingo for team meetings, she typed "put him in a literal circle"; but, oddly, she held fast to the keyboard and wouldn't allow her mother to support her typing any further. Finally, the group confirmed that "the only way they [the presences] can control is fear."

On June 27, Cindy and I arranged to visit Ryland again. Upon nearing my destination, a nearby temperature reading on a local bank says 99 and my car thermostat reads 101 degrees. Before entering the home, we joined hands in a prayer of protection, that I lead, after which Cindy added her individual intentions. En route, Cindy said that a therapist, who was scheduled to be there, called off and wouldn't be attending; he had received a midnight phone call that a client's mother and her boyfriend had both overdosed and died. (When Cindy had previously told him about our protocol for supporting Ryland, the therapist had remarked, without any prompting, that he sensed something "evil" in the house.)

Meeting with Ryland, we created a list of all the ways Ryland knows he is protected so that he can refer to it when he feels anxious. He identified his mother and father; God and Jesus; his dogs (good watchdogs, he said); a police officer who lived down the road; the mark I left on his forehead (which he told me his grandmother described as a blessing, which I affirm, "It was intended as a blessing from me to you"); a teacher at school Ryland says is the only person at school who understands him; an uncle that he doesn't see often, but feels good being with nonetheless (we focused on calling up the emotion of that sensation); his brother; and a cousin. In all, he devised 10 items on his list. We then discussed my friend's suggestion about creating a literal circle. Mark from the group had contacted me about creating a strung-together circle of hearts with loving sayings on them that could be placed around Ryland's bed for protection. Ryland agreed and Cindy was prepared by bringing crayons and construction paper with her in the car.

At about this time, I sensed such a radiant warmth and compassion emanating from the center of the informal circle in which we are all arranged. Cindy later told me—not one to pick up on body language—that Ryland must've felt it too as she noticed him close his eyes, tip his head back, and breathe deeply for a moment, as if savoring the sensation and drinking it in fully.

Finally, Ryland and I discussed the nature of "spirits" versus "ghosts." I shared with him a blow-up of the spirit photo referenced in my book *Autism and the God Connection*, and Cindy explained the meaning of the phrase "off the record" by reinforcing to Ryland that he is not alone as she, too, had seen and sensed things stretching back to her childhood.

Before departing, I was clear in telling Ryland "Love is the antidote."

In the car, we debriefed the meeting, and I was surprised to learn from Cindy that she sensed something untoward in the room in addition to the wave of compassion I felt; I was so focused on connecting with Ryland and delivering to him the best of what I knew to offer that I was oblivious to a cold draft that apparently passed through the room, felt by her (and another staff person, too, as Cindy later reported to me). In addition both staff people had noticed that the ceiling fan in the room in which we met began to "wobble" and the velocity of the blades slowed. (Cindy, noticing this, said a prayer for us all, after which the fan righted itself—later the experience was described as "weird" by someone else present at the time.) Cindy also shared that, when she went out to get the craft materials from her car, she felt a definite cold spot by the front door—this on a day with temperatures close to 100 degrees in a house without air conditioning (Ryland shared that upstairs it was even more humid).

As Cindy was concerned about what happens after each time we hold a positive gathering, she pulled over behind a processing plant so that we might join hands again to pray for Ryland and his family's protection. By July 15, I heard from Ryland and his grandmother: "I wanted to let you know that we are praying almost every evening now and it has had a positive affect on both Ryland and his brother."

November 13, 2007

I have a consultation today in a county that neighbors Ryland's county. En route, my stomach felt queasy, and I said to Amanda, the agency staff person accompanying me, "What is going on in that house?" referring to the home of our client, Trevor, age 3. Amanda said she thought there was some family stress.

Upon arriving, we were welcomed inside by Trevor and his mom, Karen. Trevor "passes" for normal, and played intently with his Thomas the Tank train set as he interacted with Amanda, and I sat and observed. After about five minutes, I asked Karen if I could speak with her privately. We moved to a formal living room area, and I told her how gorgeous her son is and how acutely sensitive he is also. I said I felt he had a lot of anxiety and friction inside, and that he needed lots of information about what's coming next, all of which she affirmed. I asked how he sleeps and she said he's better now that he's on the casein-free/gluten-free diet, but he still has problems. I asked if he awakes between midnight and 3 a.m., and she said "3 a.m." I then asked if he awakens screaming, agitated and upset; she said that he has night terrors and gets so hysterical that only holding him and rocking quells it. He ends up sleeping with her and her husband Derrick (whom I also met when he came home and joined us midway).

I told them he was acutely sensitive, and I was even wary of him overhearing us; Karen concurred, and said he can hear from across the house. I asked if she had any history on the house, and she did not. I explained that being exquisitely sensitive means filtering out nothing, and I gave my own example. I asked if she understood where I was going with this, and she did, so I said, "Okay, now let's have a frank discussion."

We began talking about the ability to perceive all things seen and unseen, and she mentioned Trevor's friend Nick, who had been someone who adored him and could calm him; he passed and appears to still visit Trevor. Karen had been wary of this and asked, to herself, "Who or what is it?" and she was impressed with the thought "It's Nick." She also glimpsed him out of the corner of her eye. She explained that her 13-year-old daughter, who might be bipolar, also wakes up screaming on occasion in response to my question about any of the other children being affected.

She told me that psychic sensitivity runs in her family, and during our conversation (when she was distressed) the phone rang and it was her mother (this happens between them often). She had been told her son needs to be on Risperdal.

She asked me to come with her to his room to see if I "got" anything. At the top of the stairs, my stomach dropped again. Trevor's room was directly before us. I asked her to step out of the room so I could step inside; I then asked if I could say a prayer, which I did. I hugged her good-bye and told her to follow up with me through Amanda if need be.

November 19, 2007

While doing a consultation for 7-year-old Andrew, I got the impression that he is very sensitive, so I asked how he was sleeping; his mother said he sleeps between she and her husband. We started talking about what he is afraid of, and when I asked him a second time, the phone rang immediately after I got the words out. It played "Old McDonald" and persisted in ringing for such an unusually prolonged period of time that Alex's dad asked his wife if it wasn't supposed to only ring four times before kicking over into the answering service. It disrupted the meeting. Afterward, my agency escort said it freaked her out, and she asked if I thought it was coincidence.

November 21, 2007

Phone consultation regarding Ronnie, a 5 year old who doesn't go to sleep until he exhausts himself at midnight, wets the bed, and has an "imaginary" friend. He experiences lots of anxiety about bedtime.

December 5, 2007

On-site consultation with Monica, an agency staff person, during which 4-year-old Shaun is hyeractive and jumping off stairs, furniture, won't bond with me—extreme state of agitation. When he goes upstairs, I'm talking with Monica, stumped; I'm talking about re-envisioning the way his schedule is used, pain and discomfort, and communication (I had showed him my portable keyboard but he wasn't interested), when out of the corner of my eye I notice the family's computer screen-saver is a slide show of family photographs. In the majority of pictures of Shaun and his older brother (who is not autistic but extremely sensitive) there are orbs—some very large and multiple in number.

I call mom, Lynn, in to speak privately and we focus on one of the many photos, and I ask her to tell me what she sees. She tells me she sees her son who is beautiful and bright—things she might expect I'd want to hear. I tell her to take a closer look and tell me now what she sees...she's confused until I point to a large orb. Lynn is a self-professed clean-buff, so we knew it wasn't reflections from air-borne dust particles (she was amused when I said this). She calls her husband, Kent, over and we do the same thing. He starts bringing up many photos—all except the most recent photos have multiple orbs. Recently, Shaun has had very bad experiences at a Christian day care, and Lynn and Kent pulled him out (it got to the point where the day care had a priest come in to observe Shaun). I asked if he's waking up between midnight and 3 a.m., and they said yes; he's terrified, and needs someone to sleep with him. I also asked about tension and stress in the household, and Lynn affirmed this (Monica later told me they are in marriage counseling). Lynn also said that they've always attended Catholic Church but, just recently, Shaun ran down the aisle up to the altar and threw his arms around the priest and wouldn't let go. She said she was advised to put Shaun on Risperdal, which she refused to do.

Brink, the family dog, was also very anxious and needed constant attention and reassurance from me. I told them that, based on the photographs, their family clearly had a protective presence about them (Lynn felt it was her father and reports seeing an unusual white moth at times), but that ill-intended presences feed from Shaun's vulnerability (people talking about him, very poor treatment in day care) and the strife within the household. Parents both have read *Autism and the God Connection*. Monica tells me that mother-in-law, who often watches Shaun, is very religious; Shaun does best in her home. She taught him to bless himself, and he had been doing this after each session of treatment drills, but has since stopped blessing himself since he has no tolerance for table-time therapy.

December 19, 2007

Three phone consultations today:

Jason, 8, who is allowed to read Stephen King and shows signs of possible bipolar but, prior to taking Concerta, was waking in the night, and now reports seeing blood stains, murdered people, and has voices calling to him.

Darren, who complains of an unseen presence, sees "monsters," has night terrors (sleeps with parents) despite bedtime sensory accommodations, and was witnessed running into an "invisible" barrier that knocked him to the floor. He has been deteriorating and shows signs of depressive symptoms including thoughts of self-harm. Psychiatrist has dismissed depression, and an opportunity to counsel family is pending.

I later learned Darren's family is in denial and has pressured him into also denying he still has such experiences, but his conduct reflects otherwise; he is now swearing at classroom peers and physically aggressing against them, he is scratching his own face, and continues to have sleep disturbances. His parents are trying to wean him back into his own bed (he's up all night when in his room). He is on the verge of being expelled from his Catholic school.

Preston's grandmother, who is raising him, reported unusual disturbances in their home especially with inconsistent electrical service; an electric repairman told her that in 30 years, it was the first time he could not pinpoint the problem.

January 30, 2008

Follow-up visit with Trevor, his mother, Karen, and father, Derrick. En route, I was talking with Amanda about the importance of protecting oneself prior to going to visit any home in which acute spirit activity is suspected. When I thought about it, I feel like something attached prior to the start of the new year. I had been very irritable, thinking lots of negative, hateful, intrusive thoughts. My dog also freaked out a couple nights, like she trembles during a storm, which caused me to bless the house.

Amanda confided that she felt something had previously followed her home from Trevor's, and that her youngest daughter, 2, was awakening during the night screaming and could not be comforted. Once Amanda prayed over her, the activity ceased.

At the house, Trevor was playing cars with his older half-brother. He showed me a monster/robot-like creature and made a point of telling me it had "red eyes."

Derrick and Karen indicated that they had been implementing my prior recommendations and things improved, but with the holidays, they slacked off and things got worse. Trevor seemed depressed and self-deprecating—lots of statements like "You don't love me" (this started after implementation of a family ritual to reinforce love among one another), and spikes of physical aggression—very out-of-character for him.

Also, electricity was being manipulated in the house: lights turning on and off, and a daughter found a light bulb outdoors that shattered in her hand as she brought it inside.

Karen said her father, staying with them, had a dream in which he saw the entities (about 10), and that they were surprised that someone could see them. They asked him what he was doing here.

Trevor has been saying he'd seen something like a black figure with red eyes. While on a recent trip to the zoo, he saw a peacock and asked Karen if it was "evil" because its eyes were red; she was stunned that, at 3, he would know the word *evil*.

They indicated that Clarissa, the family dog, was not only more clingy, but sought comfort from Derrick—unusual for her, as she shies from men.

Physical symptoms of unease are in several family members; no one can sleep comfortably in Trevor's room (Karen reported a cold spot in or near the room). We discussed empowering him with something tangible like a squirt gun. Karen said they tried giving him Febreeze air freshener to ward against the "monsters" as they're calling them; he sprayed so much that it overwhelmed the house!—an indication of how much he felt the need to use it.

When I mentioned that, en route, I said a prayer but found myself halting and blocking, Amanda said she experienced the same thing on the ride over, and Karen said she's found herself having to start over several times when saying prayers as well.

Upon leaving my legs felt a bit weak, my chest a bit heavy, and my stomach slightly queasy.

January 31, 2008

Early this morning, about 4:30 a.m., my dog was up with me and began trembling with fear as she does during a storm, but there was no storm or even high wind outside. She appeared to be looking off to one side of the room. When I put my hand on her to quell her, I conjured images of times when I felt a loving bond with her and she began to calm, but ultimately I had to put her in her crate so I could go back to bed and sleep.

March 4, 2008

On-site consultation this afternoon to meet with Monica (staff person) and 20-year-old client, Stephen, who has persisted in indicating to her that he has a presence named Zero around him that he cannot hear or see, but senses.

Prior to departure, I said a prayer of protection for us all; the trip was two hours in the pouring rain and, nearer to my destination, a deer narrowly jumped in front of the car and leapt over the guard-rail.

Interviewing Stephen, I held firm (but gently) to my beliefs that anything other than a loving presence was malignant and possessed its own agenda. He was defensive and bristled when I described such presences as *parasitic*. When I listed the ways an ill-intended presence might manifest, I suggested sleep disturbance and there was a noticeable shift in his facial expression, almost a smirk. I was very cautious about my phrasing as I sensed he might become physically agitated, and at one point he reached in his pocket but pulled out a cross on a chain that, when he departed, he allowed to drop and dangle from his hand. Yet when I said Christ was my ally, he disagreed.

He said Zero is with him for life now, and is the opposite of him and that he (Stephen) is a good person; he also described kicking a demon out of his life that, as a result, is now missing an arm and a foot. It had approached him about recruiting Stephen to "Hell's Army."

He told Monica that Zero was "curious" about me, and that when I walked in the building, he sensed an angelic presence around me, but later recanted saying Zero was disappointed that I didn't have a similar presence with me.

He said that Zero was afraid once and precluded him from entering a church wedding.

Afterward, Monica explained that Stephen's parents are divorcing. Zero apparently "woke up" from a dormant state about the time of all the tension and angst at home. Stephen was now talking about Zero tenfold, had "zoned" out in public with Monica due to Zero, and had no motivation to better himself through education or a job. He denied being intruded upon or manipulated.

Stephen doesn't fit manic symptoms (including grandiosity) and we discussed looking into a true personality disorder in addition to my theories about a spiritual attachment.

March 10, 2008

Two phone consultations with spiritual implications:

Seven-year-old Michael has been waking up as early as 11 p.m., and as late as after 3 a.m. every night with night terrors for the past couple months. (Curiously, immediately before going into the consultation, I was reading an Internet autism-parent message board thread on this very topic!) There has been a spike in his hyperactivity and anxiety; he refuses to discuss it other than to say he has nightmares, so I recommended that they try asking him to *draw* it instead to see if that helps. There is tension in the household with mother's chronic illness, Michael's complex and complicated medical conditions, and financial issues that led to the electricity being cut off in January. After extensive and recent dental surgery, it is reported that Michael seems "a little happier" (so it's likely not a pain issue), and there have been no medication changes (so no new side-effects). The family also engages in routines prior to bedtime. When Michael wakes up terrified, he sleeps with mom and dad; once asleep, they carry him back to his own bed.

Missing pieces to investigate include: Is he anxious or complaining as bedtime approaches? Is there any self-injury or increased aggression? What's he eating at dinner or before bedtime (that is, food side-effects)? Is the family dog more anxious or clingy concurrent with Michael's night terrors? (Later in the month, I received an update: "Followed up with illustrating dreams. Michael asked parents to pray with him to get rid of nightmares. They were then gone. 'God killed monster'—per Michael.")

Next was a long phone consultation (third-time regarding this client) with Cathy about 12-year-old Elizabeth. Her Prozac had been decreased and her Abilify (used to treat schizophrenia and manic episodes of bipolar) had been discontinued. I sent Cathy my list of medication alternatives for Elizabeth's family, who is not keen on medication. I reinforced the importance of defining depressive symptoms with Cathy. She has already done this by interviewing Elizabeth and her mother separately. Cathy felt Elizabeth was guarded, withholding information; when discussing depression with her mother, Elizabeth meets most every symptom.

Lately, Elizabeth has been opening up to Donna, a therapist, about what staff is describing as "imaginary friends" whom Elizabeth says have been with her since she was 2 or 3 years old, but recently have become prominent in her life (pre-adolescence). There are a number of entities she describes including three "vampire" children—a family of siblings—aged 8, 11, and 12. The 12-year-old is Gregory, with whom she is closest, and whom she wants to marry (even describing the colors of her bridal gown). They come out at night, according to Elizabeth, and, because she sleeps in the basement and her parents sleep on another floor, her parents don't have a sense of whether Elizabeth is up during the night or not, though it seems likely.

When Cathy shared that Gregory told Elizabeth not to take her Abilify because it makes him "go away" and to tell her parents it upsets her stomach so it can be discontinued, I started to question how Elizabeth could've fabricated something like that. As I began this piece of the discussion, the phone line started to cut out and I was disconnected; when I called back, the line still was not clear, so it required Cathy calling me back.

In addition to the vampire family, there is also "Any C" an "angel of God." (The "C" stands for "cat" or "child.") Any C has given Elizabeth a magic wand with instructions to use it to bless people or kill them as she sees fit. If used to kill them, she may do it slowly, or put them out of their misery by killing them swiftly. She has drawn pictures of the wand and in some, it has a sharp, pointed tip and in others, it looks like a scythe with blood dripping from it. Any C told Elizabeth that she is permitted to show the wand to staff within three days (which would be tomorrow). There's also Johnny C and Johnny the Homicidal Maniac, who seem to have their roots in anime. Cathy said that the entities at first started out as "light" fairies, but became progressively darker, and there has been a spike in Elizabeth's physical aggression at school—she has attacked at least one boy.

Because some of what has been described sounds like the grandiosity aspect of mania, I requested that Cathy review manic symptoms, but when we did it verbally by phone, no other symptoms fit. I also wondered if there might be a true personality disorder present. In addition, we talked about how Elizabeth perceives her experience as authentic, and Cathy said she thought it was authentic. I suggested we determine the next steps after a review of mental health symptoms.

Also on this date, I received an e-mail from Jackie, who writes of a persuasive presence from her childhood:

> When I was a little girl I had invisible friends. That's not so unusual; what's unusual is the reactions that they got from other people. Mr. Nobody (he asked me for a name, and I gave him one) was much taller than people, wore clothing that was out of date for the time, had long, black hair all over his body, and stank—much like a cross between a 15-year-old that isn't careful about hygiene, and a Billy goat. If it wasn't for his apparent, slouchy youth and his old-style clothing, I would call him a satyr.
>
> I visited him out in the woods, and played with him during many afternoons. There was one time we stole the car,

and another time he came into the house. Other people could smell him, but didn't see him.

I assumed he was a product of my fertile imagination except that my sister, many years later, said that "when you went to school, Mr. Nobody would balance out the see-saw when we played." Later on I asked about the car I went for a joyride in. It wasn't a standard. It was a clutch. I am, to this day, very tiny—how could I have operated that huge car at the time? I still don't know.

I have lots of reasons to believe that I imagined him, but some parts of what I remember don't fit neatly, such as why a little girl would choose an imaginary 6-and-a-half-foot boy as a playmate.

I was officially diagnosed ADHD when I was 7, and I'm 44 now. I am confidant that today I would have earned a high-functioning autism diagnosis, like my son and my younger brother have. When my son, Nikko, was 3—before he talked even—he picked up the phone before I could get to it. He listened, and hung up. He said, clear as you would expect a 3-year-old to speak, "Mr. Nobody wants you to know that he is real and that he is coming for you."

RECRUITMENT RISING

In reflection of the events just recounted, I am reminded of Stephen's admission that a demon had attempted to recruit him for service in Hell's Army. Stephen's demon was named "Zero," but others have had equally ambiguous monikers: "No Name," "Mr. Nobody," and "Any C." One Florida mother wrote that after a visit to the cemetery, her young son with autism "said on the way home something was following us, it was *no one who came from nowhere*. It was not a person, but it was bad. We have pictures of what people call orbs, but the (picture) of the window of the van shows a face with teeth. He was pretty scared." "No one who came from nowhere," in addition to the other persona non-grata identities, reminded me very much of *The Exorcist* and the demon who, upon replaying the audio tape in reverse, communicates, *"I am no one."* It appears that such acrimonious minions are so lacking in esteem and self-value—so enmeshed in twisted servitude to the Great Deceiver are they—that they disparage the authenticity of individuality.

Our culture persists in portraying the pathology and purported deficit-based nature of autism. If what one with autism has experienced becomes pervasive, it makes sense that malicious entities would target autistics because they're already vulnerable to everyone's disbelief, indifference, or disregard—which only paves the way to increased agitation or, worse yet, physical aggression, in attempts to communicate their terrifying experiences. This is precisely the plan of such malevolent forces, as described by one mom from Wisconsin in a desperate e-mail to me:

> I am a mother of a 7-year-old son with autism, Jeff. At age 4, he began seeing angels during Mass, especially at the time of consecration. At first I thought he meant the altar boys, and asked him, "Do you mean the boys like David (his older brother)?" and he said no. Then he went on to say they stand around the altar and are bigger than Father Gerard (our priest who's 6-foot, 2-inches tall). This has gone on every other Sunday or so for two-plus years.
>
> Then suddenly this past month he began being scared at church and has said, "There is someone evil in the pew, I'm scared." Last Sunday (Divine Mercy Sunday) was terrible. I walked into church and he got stiff as a board and began sweating and breathing fast. I went into the "cry room" with him and my other two boys, and he started *screaming*, "It's evil! It's so evil, I'm scared!" So, in the interest of those who were there to attend Mass, I got him ready to leave, and he began kicking and screaming and went for my throat! I live a block from church, and when I got home he went right to my bed and slept until the next day! He was completely exhausted!

I've noticed the mounting propensity of some children and teens (autistic or otherwise) who are drawn to "dark" aspects of films, video games, and music—which may predispose one to pornography, crime, addiction, and abuse. I'm left pondering the concept of a spiritual warfare and a recruitment for Hell's Army, as Stephen had described it, by implanting a nefarious, nesting seed in the vulnerable minds of our young people. This may be especially true given the generations of increasing numbers of children with autism who are altruistic and spiritually gifted. Are they under attack and at risk of being psychically brainwashed to do harm instead of good? My friend Julia, mom to son, Adam, offered her perspective:

> I also have been hearing a lot of sensitive kids who are part of the "ADHD era" being more prone to violence, and saying that they are seeing "demons" (my oldest son included but we have "fixed" that), and hearing voices. It's almost like they are being recruited in some sense. I know that seems very "Sci-Fi Channel" but from firsthand experience, at least four children of the pre-teens in my neighborhood were all grouped into the ADD category and all were recently involved in a neighborhood crime; they all reported seeing the exact same figure before they became aggressive or got into trouble.
>
> My next-door neighbor's child, who is adopted and is on the (autism) spectrum, was telling me for the longest time that he was seeing a "demon in a graveyard" every time right before something bad happened at school or he lost his temper. Being me, I asked him if he believed in God and he said, "No." I said, "Then you need to pray and I will pray for you." When he told me of this figure, the word *adversary* came into my head and I did not understand what that meant. I read the Bible, but I can't quote it from memory, and I don't understand a lot of what's in it. But upon consulting with another sensitive friend of mine, who does know the Bible inside out, she told me that adversary was the correct term for the Devil's (or whatever word you want to call it) "recruiter" so to speak.
>
> Well, after I prayed for this poor child, he told me that he had an incident at school the next day where he got

angry at another child and right before he would have gotten into a fight with him, he saw this figure again. However,
before the figure could "speak" to him, purple lightning
started to strike between him and the figure, and he (the
child) passed out at school. Divine intervention perhaps?
I know that purple is a divine color and for it to appear
in that context is pretty powerful. Unfortunately this poor
child was not allowed to come over and hang out with my
oldest son anymore because he went home and told his
parents that he was seeing things, and what I told him to
do about it, and they kept him housebound and put him on
anti-psychotic medicine which made him worse. He wound
up getting in with this group of other neighborhood children and got into trouble for breaking into homes and is
now in juvenile detention. Such a waste; he is a very smart
child but is very misunderstood and his parents sadly did
not get him the help he needed until too late.

But he would come over to our house every day and
sit on our front porch because he said it was the only place
he felt safe and that he never saw any "bad stuff" while he
was at our house. I wish I could help them all. I wish parents
were more open to the idea of spiritualism —our children are
a prime target for the good and the bad—but they need
to be educated on how to empower themselves to know
the difference.

POWER STRUGGLE

As a pre-adolescent, I also developed what became an unhealthy
fascination for deviant subject matter: witches, ghosts, vampires, and
the like, and, later, *The Exorcist* and similar films. As a child, with what
I know now was Asperger's Syndrome, I was always trying to find ways
to "fit in." This often meant becoming someone other than who I was
because who I was wasn't working. While still in elementary school, I
began exploring books about the supernatural. My adult suspicion is
that, at this age more than ever (and on the precipice of adolescence),
any child is vulnerable to being persuaded by dark elements. I soon

developed a red, discolored pigmentation in the palm of my right hand that no doctor could explain or remedy. In later years, my mother candidly observed that, at the time, she was concerned it was some sort of "mark." (As an adult, I was stunned to learn that such a mark is referenced in the Book of Revelation.)

At this point, my parents curtailed my disturbing indulgences, but I surreptitiously continued. I imagined that I had "powers" and presented myself this way to classmates and others. I told them that, at night, I sprouted bat wings and flew about my room. I even invited them to feel the "nubs" on my shoulders. I fantasized that my powers could exact revenge upon my bullies and tormentors.

Once, on the playground, some other children challenged me to *prove it*, to which I replied, "How?" One boy urged me to cause a spell to break up a large, multi-boy fistfight that was occurring within our view. I began to mumble some hitherto incantation and I was no sooner finished when, at that precise moment, a strong gust of wind reeking of cow manure swept over the entire playground. It not only succinctly broke up the fight, it sent *everyone* scattering for cover. The event was a turning point. Not only did my classmates now believe in my powers, I began to believe them myself. Clearly "someone" was sending this message—but not without a price.

Being very rigid in my thinking, I associated witchcraft exclusively with Satan, and, at this time, I was ripe for being marked as a potential disciple. I enjoyed the renewed public attention I garnered but, privately, I also knew it was a trade-off. Every night before falling asleep, I "thought" I could hear footsteps coming closer and closer to my bedroom door. Or was it the beating of my own heart pressed against my pillow? I tried saying the Lord's Prayer, but violent or pornographic images crowded my head instead. Then the footsteps stopped, and, in my mind, I saw a very tall, dark figure in a long floor-length coat and a large brimmed hat standing in my doorway—black and imperceptible because of the light behind him. Without words, I understood he was there to seduce me into seriously consummating what I had started as innocent play, and advance it to the next level. And every night, in my mind, I had to refuse him countless times until he faded from view... until the next night. The ritual of resisting this dark presence continued for quite some time. But, eventually, the vision—and the mark on my palm—mercifully dissipated completely away.

In *The Ascent to Truth* (Harvest Books, 2002), monk Thomas Merton suggests that outside agents, both good and impure, could impress "pictures" or visions of supernatural things upon our imaginations, writing, "The Devil...has the power to make you see things and think things as he wants you to see and think them." My experience was not unlike that of other youth lured and wrongly dissuaded by the dark influence of harmful, abusive activities, narcotics, alcohol, or music with violent themes. (In *Autism and the God Connection*, I examine in depth the pathway to finding myself and retrieving my own spiritual faith following this period.)

More than 20 years later, I worked with a man with whom I felt comfortable enough to discuss spiritual issues. I risked sharing with him my childhood struggles with what I imagined as a dark force attempting to indoctrinate me into its legions. After I finished, the man related to me a similar story about his two sons who, when young, shared a bedroom and for some time were terrified at night by a presence outside their window. So adamant were they that, at one point, the man scattered sawdust on the ground outside to capture footprints to no avail. Then my friend related the boys' description of the presence: both described a tall, dark man with a long, floor-length coat and black hat—and red, glowing eyes. What brought me to tears in that moment was that—up until that point—I had always chalked up my experience to pure imagination. Later, with the advent of the Internet, a Wikipedia search for the phrase "shadow people" (prompted by an autistic client's complaints of such in his home) depicted an illustration of what is an apparent universally-seen phantom: *a tall, dark figure in a brimmed hat and long coat.*

THE ANTIDOTE

The sole antidote to counteract presences of ill-intent is *LOVE*. Love is a high-vibration emotion that, in its purity and simplicity, trumps all negative, low-vibration emotions. Parents and caregivers are encouraged to identify family stressors while respectfully ascertaining family faith and spirituality. By building upon family values, we may encourage or reinforce the importance of family faith. During this time, families may decide to recommit attending religious services or having their home blessed. Although this should *not* be discouraged, it is not enough and oftentimes a blessing of the home has little effect because the person conducting the blessing is not emotionally invested in the family. The blessing is not the antidote—the antidote is love within a family united. (Moving away is not a solution either. Bodiless and devoid of physical constraints, the plaguing entities have the ability to go wherever they wish simply by conceptualizing it. Once they latch onto the very sensitive vibrations of the individual with autism, they will follow wherever he or she may go. Trust me, I've seen it happen.)

Additionally, families are encouraged to *consistently* implement the following protocol (an inconsistent, hit-or-miss approach is not enough):

* Establish a clear, consistent, and predictable schedule for bringing closure to the day's activities as a family.
* Use bathtime as an opportunity to destress and calm by using soft lighting, favored music, and scented bathwater.
* Gather together as a family to discuss the day's events and reinforce the unity of the family bonded in love and support of one another.
* Validate each other's place and role in the family, and what each contributes to the unity of the family unit.
* Join together in prayer or meditation.
* Bless the house and, particularly, the individual's bedroom.
* Pray for protection of the individual.
* Pray for the unwanted presences, which will confuse and disarm them (remember they, too, originated in God).
* Empower the individual with autism with the authority to draw strength from his or her faith, and command the unwanted presences to leave.
* Make this authority tangible by providing the individual with a flashlight, squirt-gun, or religious object to ward off nighttime interruptions.
* Make the individual's bedroom as pleasing an environment as possible with attention to bedding fabrics, lighting and nighlights, and soothing music.

* Know that love within a family united *will* create more and more positive emotion that will benefit the entire family, also creating less and less negative emotion, which feeds the spiritual assault or "attachment."

RETALIATION

I feel quite confident in stating that I am one of the most honest people you could ever wish to meet. I don't lie about anything, *ever*—not even what other people call "little white lies." Instead, I say what I mean and mean what I say. I may not choose to reveal the entire truth of a given matter, and, through the years, I've learned to articulate difficult dialogue with a measure of diplomacy, but I always tell the truth as I know it to be. This position has also required me to be very careful and thorough in giving an accounting of myself by reflecting upon my past transgressions and unsavory conduct, confronting myself with the clarity of truth, and making atonement for my previous misbehavior and shameful shortcomings. This has been a process, but a necessary one. It has also been liberating. I have no secrets and nothing to hide; everything is out in the open and every corner of my being has been fully illuminated.

As you might imagine, when discussing presences of ill intent, the attitudes I purvey about purity of self has made me quite unpopular with those very presences because they are all about cowardice, duplicity, deception, and harmful purpose. It is cowardly that these entities should prey upon, terrorize, and confuse innocent young people; it is duplicitous that they should portend an allyship under false pretenses (as in Stephen's case); it is deceptive to purvey myths and stereotypes about autism by targeting those very individuals, knowing they are not likely to be believed; and the harmful outcomes are plainly evident, as you've just read. The journey I've undertaken is something they either can't or won't do themselves. (As you've read, they are often anonymous in their own identity.) Suffice it to say, they don't like me for it; they don't like me revealing the truth to you now, and there is oftentimes a price to pay on behalf of doing so. Aside from my own insomnia, such hindrances usually take the form of minor irritations and nuisances, though if I were not so stalwart in my faith I suspect it could become far worse.

As incredible as it may sound, I take the contents of this chapter quite seriously as do countless families who also recognize the truth, but have, instead, been told their child is psychotic and in need of strong, prescriptive medication to stop the physical aggression and hallucinations. There is a mindset that anyone with autism is culpable for manifesting extreme, out-of-control behavior when, in fact, the opposite is true: we are talking about individuals who are naturally and exquisitely gentle and sensitive. Within the past year, I was made aware of a psychologist who told a family their son needed an exorcism for his aggressive conduct, and I am learning of the alarming frequency with which some families are pursuing exorcism or a religious "deliverance" ceremony. In one instance, a professional colleague told me of his meeting with Allea, a 15-year-old client with Asperger's. She apparently felt camaraderie with him enough to reveal that she and a school friend saw a recently deceased teacher outside the school on the front steps. She then said that she has grappled with the presence of a "demon" (her word). She indicated that her mother held an exorcism and that it temporarily subsided but that, in recent times, the demon has returned. She does not perceive it as harming her and missed it previously because she was "lonely." This is problematic due to the motives of some families to exorcise their child's *autism*, not to relieve symptoms of a spiritual assault. It also reinforces shameful and hurtful attitudes to the child already weakened and victimized.

If you find yourself questioning the veracity of my claims, please know that most people on the autism spectrum interpret what they perceive very *literally*. Although we are not void of imagination no one persists in telling tales of ghosts or demons that antagonize them at night for days, weeks, or even years. (Further, hallucinations and aggressive conduct have no clinical association with the symptoms of autism.) These experiences have great potential to influence our spiritual future by furthering myths and stereotypes about the misconduct of individuals with autism *and*, if the ill-intended presences gain the upper-hand, it can permanently disable the ability for natural-born healers, empaths, and visionaries to help and heal others.

I am only too willing to empower others with the strength to openly discuss these issues such as Christopher, a precocious 11-year-old who, at our initial introduction, began our consultation by magnanimously stating his top priority, "When I'm alone, I don't feel like I'm alone. I feel like I'm being watched and it's not a good feeling." My calm assurances led to a greater discussion about his perceptive capacity, and he has soared in his self-advocacy and desire to educate about the autism spectrum.

I am convinced that if families under siege will enact my antidote things *will* improve—I've been witness to it on many occasions. But it requires *work and commitment* and, when it comes to autism, too many parents have been led to believe that regulated interactions with their child are the responsibility of a qualified professional. (If I am the one who is autistic, then who is better qualified to make things right within my very home than my own mom and dad!) Case in point, not long ago I consulted for a family that met my criteria for a spiritual attack involving their young son. During my interview, the mother was also forthcoming in sharing that she had been imbibing alcohol with increasing frequency—an addiction that becomes a conductor which facilitates the vicious cycle. The family immediately adhered to my protocol (which included abstaining from liquor) and, when I followed up 48 hours later, I learned that their son had slept soundly for two consecutive nights for the first time in many weeks. But, when vacationing at the shore soon afterward, the mother frantically emailed me to report that things had fallen apart. In passing, she mentioned that she had resumed drinking socially as well. I was angered: the protocol requires a commitment that includes self-discipline, not a when-you-feel-like-it implementation.

Further, once the antidote is implemented, things may, indeed, get worse before they get better. *This is a test.* I never said this would be easy, and if it was, families would never learn the strength of their conviction and the depth of their love. There may, in fact, be retaliation by the spiteful energies in resistance to the unification of a family bonded in love. Love is a threat to them, and I am reminded of all the times I've observed electricity, computers, and telephones go haywire in times of my counseling teams with heartfelt compassion. Recall, too, Ryland's shattered ceiling fan and my near-miss collision with a deer. (As you've also read, my mood has been negatively affected.) Recently, upon arriving home from empowering a family with this new knowledge, I discovered that some metal parts to my basement weight set, stowed up high on a cabinet top, had inexplicably scattered to the cellar floor and my computer's power box had malfunctioned, though the computer was unplugged in my absence. Still, do not be afraid. Trust, have faith, and know that true love conquers all. As proof of such empowerment, here's more from Julia about young Adam's glorious resolve:

> He saw a dark hooded figure…I told him that if he could control the initial "fear" then he would be able to tell if the person was positive or negative and that *he had control* over the experience. He could tell this person to leave. He still has issues with this, but he is able now to be casual about it. He will just say, "I'm going to bed now and you need to leave."

PART THREE

FUTURE FORECASTS

Chapter 6

A Remarkable Revelation

"God tells me truth."
—Message typed to the author by David
upon being introduced to him in his group home.

Allow me to preface the last part of this book by reiterating a position that often gets muddied and misinterpreted (especially by reviewers): I do not presume to be writing about—or representing—*all* persons on the autism spectrum; this is why I have always been careful to use the words *many*, *most*, and *some*, not *every* or *all*. I am, instead, making probable generalizations based upon my opinion and my experience knowing full well that I do not speak for everyone. In the Asperger's community, self-advocates seem somewhat divided when it comes to the topic of spirituality and instances of giftedness, based on message-board postings I've read on the topic. Their comments have included, "I feel no connection at all to any of those things. I am a realist that does not believe in things that aren't proven," "Deeply agnostic, leaning hard toward skepticism when it comes to anything 'supernatural,'" and "Do I have a connection with spirituality? Yes, very much so. Do I have a connection with something beyond? I'm skeptical of the possibility, but also open to it." (In my most cynical era, I would've once bitterly criticized it all as bunk myself.) For the most part, these are people who do not have frequent and ongoing interaction with families, caregivers, and individuals with autism as do I, and have only their own lives as a point of reference. As with the mainstream population, one's ability to be open-minded to unlimited possibilities is either instilled from childhood, cultivated with maturity,

127

affirmed by personal experience, tempered in accordance with religious beliefs, or all of the above.

As part of thorough research for my spiritual work, I came to learn that there are nearly 500 Biblical passages that cite seers and prophets (in mostly positive ways) who were valued for their ability to foretell future events; in defending such modern-day events, a quote that has become a favorite of mine is St. John, 14:12, in which Jesus says, "He that believeth on me, the works that I do shall he also do; and greater works than these shall he do..." In my interpretation Christ is referring to the untapped potential of humankind to match *and exceed* the divine capacity of Jesus for being of good and great service to others through the employ of our individual spiritual gifts and talents. (For those who are not of Christian faith, let me also add that, for me, personally, believing whether or not Jesus was the son of God is not as important as my desiring to emulate the example he set.)

Also as part of research, I happened upon a Website, JewishFuture.com, which I found most intriguing. It was created shortly after the terrorist attacks of September 11, 2001, and tells of a number of young men and women with autism of Jewish faith who are considered severely impaired but, through typing their communications, have revealed some startling insights about the human race and where things are heading. Their forecasts make for interesting contrast with the comments from some opposing persons with Asperger's, and are prefaced by the following statement that is much in keeping with the contentions I've advanced:

All of us have higher spiritual parts to our being. Some people are more sensitive to the higher self—and some people live their lives completely unaware. But it has been observed that some autistic people have an unusually active higher self. Because "nature" has a looser grip on an autistic mind, the spiritual parts of the autist are able to go to higher places, free of the burden of normal physical existence.

We give this preface to set the stage for the articles [on the Website]. They are the words of several autistic students in Jerusalem, Israel, and in America. And though these students are normally not able to speak due to their level of autism, they are able to communicate with others through a method called Facilitated Communication. The messages they have been giving, or "revealing" over the past 10 years strongly suggest (clearly state) we are at the brink of a major upheaval in the world community.

A review of the students' messages (the most recent date from 2007) reveals unanimous consensus for an impending time of global human suffering and great miracles followed by a period of redemption—all from the perspective of Jewish faith. Detailed advisements are also provided by the students with regard to preparing for the ensuing wars through spiritual means (which include renouncing sinful ways) and by physical means (preserving and storing food and water as in any emergency). Binyamin is passionate when he states, "The only protection is to be closely attached to God." Batya, 16 at the time of her 2001 writings, is as equally assertive in her writings: "We are constantly receiving messages. Not only from the mentally handicapped people, but also directly from God…Whoever is smart, opens his eyes, observes what is going on, and understands that God is bringing the end. The end of the world as we know it…. There are prophesies which state that few Jews will survive to greet Moshiach, but there is an alternative and this depends on our deeds."

It would seem as though if ever there were a time when we could mark the beginning of the end, it would've initiated with the events of September 11. But what struck me was the notion of people with autism having the vision to prophesize the "end of days" for the rest of us. I had already covered instances of premonition that some with autism had for the safety of their immediate family, like the numerous occasions that a child "tantrumed" in the car, compelling the family to make an unplanned pit-stop, only to find they would've been the epicenter of a multi-car pileup had they stayed the course. In another example, a mom shared her son's illustrations (rendered in the days preceding September 11) of a series of clocks, all set to 9:11. The same child had also drawn a fiery crash in a wooded glade. What to make of autism and prophecy, I pondered. I hadn't given it thought beyond a few scattered anecdotes, but might there be a bigger picture to unveil?

Granted, it's a tricky subject and one that, unless handled respectfully and delicately, has the potential to be more a disservice than a way to serve people with autism. In the interim, I tucked the idea away and pursued other topics that might seem less volatile and more prudent.

THE GRAND SCHEME

Then, in the spring of 2007, I enjoyed a private chat with my dear friend, Renee, a young woman with Down syndrome and autism who doesn't often speak but, instead, types on a portable keyboard with physical support at the wrist from her mother. On this particular afternoon, Renee was affirming my speculations about autism as a component of human evolution and that persons with autism who live in silence are oftentimes keepers of extraordinary wisdom. Then the conversation shifted in a direction previously unconsidered by me. She began to share her perceptions not just about the past and present, but about *the future*. It was a remarkable revelation that immediately conjured forgotten recollections of JewishFuture.com.

I was fascinated as Renee went on to tell me that her intuition gives her great insight for placing the grand scheme of forthcoming events into proper context. To my surprise (and her mother's as well), Renee typed that, within the next century, "intellect will be elevated." There would also be economic strife "the likes of which our civilization has never seen" (note that this was well before the September 2008 stock market crash and the ensuing national economic woes), and "global warming issues Al Gore hasn't even conceived of." But, there was light and optimism too. Renee suggested that, afterward, "our people"—meaning those who are misjudged, maligned and misinterpreted as intellectually inferior—will flourish in a new humanity. (Unbeknownst to Renee, Edgar Cayce [1877-1945], the famous American prophet, indicated an impending global advancement in our overall species refinement via a series of seven emerging "root races" that corresponds with Renee's projection. Moreover, modern-day children's spirituality researcher, PMH Atwater, author of *Children of the New Millennium* and *Beyond the Indigo Children*, contends that Cayce's prediction of the fifth root race evolution will ascend in accordance with the 2012 higher-octave-of-human-vibration forecast by the Mayan calendar, leading to soaring intelligence in future generations.)

I was spellbound by Renee's thought-provoking precognitions, and began to wonder if others with autism held similar visions for the future; if so, would such visions be consistent if not synchronous? If people with autism, unknown to one another, were all sharing like sentiments it could well prove revelatory in our collective comprehension as a civilization on the brink of a great shift. I decided to pursue it further. (As an aside, those who persist in the venture to invalidate Facilitated Communication do so without consideration of assessing it on a person-by-person basis; disregard at least 11 published studies in peer-reviewed journals that verify the technique; and ignore a growing number of self-advocates who began using FC, but now type independently.)

Revisiting JewishFuture.com I uncovered a passage that lends reasoning to the inequity between many indifferent or disbelieving people with Asperger's Syndrome and those with autism who don't speak, but more readily tap their intuitive purpose in mysterious ways (italics are my emphasis), "...the Sages of the Talmud (Baba Basra 12a) hinted to this occurrence when they said that after the era of formal prophecy had ended there would still be a remnant of higher knowledge available through young children and people *of limited mental abilities* (Hebrew word: "shotim") whose minds are more loosely bound into this physical world." This very concept was the foundation for my two other books about autism and a spiritual connection—that many individuals who appear to be severely limited on the surface may actually be more conscious and aware than the average person when it came to perceiving the world through a prism of heightened sensitivity.

The challenge becomes convincing others that this is possible. As way-out-there as what I've proffered may seem, perhaps the more radical proposition is that people with autism are aware, mentally intact, and intelligent beings. Even after I had developed a questionnaire to collect relevant information from those very persons, I heard from an employee of a behavioral health facility that aids children, teens, and adults with autism, who bruskly stated, "Your survey questions are far above the ability level of the people we serve." *Baloney*, I thought! This is an issue of communication limitations imposed by a neurology compromised, not an issue of competence. (I promptly sent a copy of a document I had composed to address this very attitude, listing ways to enrich our relationships through a belief in competence.) I suspected that, the further I explored gleaning data from people with autism, the more an omission for a belief in competence would become an obstacle.

CRAFTING A QUESTIONNAIRE

To begin, I decided that a brief survey would be one way to gather information relevant to my cause: Do some very sensitive people with autism have great insight for our collective future in the same ways that Renee does or even the young autists at JewishFuture.com? It was a pursuit as tantalizing as it was voyeuristic, and, while I presupposed that the most revelatory responses would come from those individuals who live in silence, I determined to make the survey accessible to all persons on the autism spectrum regardless of age or diagnosis (in other words it mattered not whether someone was deemed low- or high-functioning).

I wanted to keep my questionnaire simple and concise yet with leeway for elaboration by each person completing it. I also thought it important that my line of questioning establish a linear sequence, beginning with the beginning (one's birth) and in the context of a relationship with God. (I felt that plunging right into, "So, what's going to happen to humankind in the future?" would come with a built-in intimidation factor, let alone seem audacious in its forwardness.) Here is my questionnaire as it was generated and disseminated:

1. What are your earliest memories of being in the world?

2. Have you always had an understanding of your place in the world?

3. Have you sensed a divine presence (such as God) close to you? If so, has it been consistent throughout your life?

4. Does this divine presence guide and inform you? If so, in what ways?

5. Do you have insights into human civilization? If so, in what ways?

6. Do you have insights into the future of our civilization? If so, in what ways?

7. Are you fearful or optimistic about your insights?

8. Do you believe your insights will manifest or are they only forecasts?

9. What can we do to guide and inform others (including non-believers) about such insights?

10. What would you wish for the average reader to understand about what you've shared?

I began to distribute the survey by following up with all those parents and persons with autism who had so generously contributed to my two previous books. I also contacted people in my e-mail address book who had responded positively to the books, and had followed up to share their own "God connections" or to graciously bestow me with their accolades—this meant they "got it" and were available to new ways of thinking. Additional sources for distribution were through networks I had with religious groups that advocated disability-inclusion for its members; holistic health practitioners and autism consultants; and Internet forums such as *Children of the New Earth*, an online magazine for inspired parenting. Slowly but surely, as the results began to trickle in, I wondered if Donald's declaration, "God tells me truth," would, in fact, bear true.

Chapter 7

Casting the Net

"When the solution is simple, God is answering."
—Albert Einstein

Pursuant to the results of my survey, and by way of background, it may be worthwhile to hold a sidebar about *how* it is that those of us on the autism spectrum come to perceive information unseen and unknown by others. You will recall, from Chapter 4, the list of the senses and the correlating stimuli that can be painfully assaultive to those so predisposed. Although the *expressive* capacity of many autistics is deemed sub-par (because they are challenged in speech articulation), their *receptive* ability—being able to receive varied communications, including that spoken—is operating at maximum capacity or, in many instances, is in overdrive. This manifests in an extension of the sensory perceptions of each exquisitely sensitive being that heightens and sharpens the acuity beyond what is typical. This can lead to receptive input to which most others are not privy. Curiously, it is in this very manner that prophets, seers, and sages also receive information—delineated in accordance with the senses, or a combination thereof. In visionary vernacular, here's how it breaks down:

* Clear Seeing = Clairvoyance
* Clear Hearing = Clairaudience
* Clear Feeling or Sensing = Clairsentience
* Clear Smelling = Clairgustance or Clairambience
* Clear Tasting = Clairalience

These so-called Gifts of the Spirit are identical to the manner in which many people with autism assimilate with the world on a daily basis. As I've noted, this way of being is not only natural to each such individual, it is also often overlooked or disregarded. Thank goodness I've awakened this ability within myself because I use it in my work. This sensitivity is what allows me to forego the regime of formal assessments or a review of IQ or psychological exams for my clients. I require only a matter of moments alone with a given individual to know their needs, and, in the absence of that person's physical presence, a snapshot will do.

For example, in spring 2008, I had a consultation in northeast Pennsylvania for 5-year-old Curtis, whom I observed briefly in school. He was actually in a small alcove (the time-out room) trying to complete math exercises on paper but was distracted, and his aide was loud and forceful. After observing him for about five minutes, I left and met with Ronald's mother in the school office. She and her husband had recently attended one of my autism presentations. She shared how very helpful it was and it prompted her husband to speculate that he had Asperger's Syndrome. When I asked her how Curtis was sleeping, she indicated that he wakes up about three nights a week screaming, and he has been increasingly anxious and agitated. I next enquired about stress or tension in the household, and she was honest and forthcoming. She was going back to school, her husband was out of work, and their only income was Curtis's Supplemental Security Insurance. She said they lived in her husband's father's house (who had passed away). He was not a nice person and she said she feels his heavy and oppressive presence in the house. In addition, Curtis's sister had an "imaginary friend." Mother had read my protocol for these events and understood Curtis's spiritual sensitivities, and that he may be sensing much negative residue in the household.

The ability for me to serve Curtis's mother in this manner, as well as others, comes from (1) being on the autism spectrum myself, (2) being sensitively attuned, and (3) thinking in pictures that relate to the situation with which I am presented in the moment.

I'll also sometimes get what I call *bleed-over*, intuitive information adjunct, but indirectly related, to a client, like the family consultation I once had in Pittsburgh. One of the family dogs would not leave me alone, and stood patiently at my feet staring at me intently. When the mother tried to redirect the dog away, I said, "No, no, it's okay. He wants to tell me something." I had the impression that the dog's stomach troubled him, and asked about that. The mother replied that, indeed, the dog had stomach issues. I asked what they were doing about that, and she said they used a prescription medication. I next had the impression that the dog desired chicken broth to soothe its stomach, so when I asked about that, the mother told me that they had given the dog chicken broth in the past. (I learned the next day that the mother had gone out that night after I left, and got the dog chicken broth!) In a follow-up, I was informed that "the dog is actually doing much better and sat by the door with his nose pressed against the door waiting for you to come back."

If you remember Magic 8-Ball from the1960s, you'll better appreciate how I get clear seeing, or clairvoyant, information. Magic 8-Ball was an oversized black-and-white pool ball replica, and the base was a transparent window through which one could glimpse the inky blue-black liquid with which it was filled. Upon making a wish or an inquiry, you shook Magic 8-Ball's contents and peered through the window for a message (supposedly relevant to the question just asked) that would mysteriously appear, rising to the surface after a second or so. This is kind of what happens in my head—I get pictures and movies and words, or sometimes I'll see a word paired with an image. I've learned to say what I see because what I see is usually spot-on accurate. Not that I assume credit for any of it, mind you—just prior to making a consultation I spend time in prayer and contemplation. I request that God use me as the conduit through which good and great information will flow, and I meditate on fulfilling the purpose that awaits me with authenticity. So natural is it for me, so accustomed have I become to operating this way, that it takes me by surprise should someone find anything to be astounded by. My point in telling all this is to provide the reader with an appreciation of how those who responded to my survey were most likely to have received the spiritual information they revealed—through one or more extrasensory attunements that correlate with the senses—though they, themselves, may not have ever realized it or given it consideration.

Results and Responses

In this section I intend to examine the responses to my survey by reflecting upon the most salient reactions to each question as I posed it. What is presented here is a sample of the results that came to me. Mind you, I am not a statistician, nor is this a scientific exercise in data-driven research; it is merely an inquisitive venture of my own quest for anecdotal supposition and introspection of a mystical nature.

The ages of the responders ranged from 7 to adults in their mid-60s. Most who responded were from the United States with a few from Germany and Australia where my books have fledgling followings. I will not be making the distinction about whether a person's diagnosis would categorize their functioning ability as "high" or "low." In my opinion, there is no such distinction—all are intelligent, capable human beings. The requests for surveys were many, but, ultimately, the returns were rather sparse (30 total), which suggests at work the common autistic hindrance of disorganization and the inability to meet deadlines. But, really, it's the quality of the information received that matters not the quantity. Spiritual inclinations aside, the responders' answers may be fascinating from the viewpoint of an alternative logic and uncommon conjecture often unique to those on the autism spectrum. Here, then, are the replies to my queries:

Question 1: What are your earliest memories of being in the world?

Anne-Laure, age 45: My earliest memories are when I was exposed to strong sensory input, for example the screaming I did when I had to wade in a thick swarm of seaweeds.

Fred, age 12: I have been here so many times as different people. I think a few thousand years ago I was the son of a woman in the area of current China. He was treated horribly to the extent that he died of malnutrition. Being Fred, my earliest memories are Mom singing to me as an infant.

George, age 11: I remember being held in my (now late) grandma's arms being rocked on a special rocking chair, which still exists in my house. I must have been around 5 months old then. She used to give me the bottle. I remember looking at my hands and noticing the wrinkles and lines on my hands then. Right now, this present moment, I sat in that rocking chair and "saw" myself of the time then. As I did that I felt her arms around me.

Izzy, age 32: I remember being with God.

James, age 16: I remember being in my mom. I remember being born. Pain and struggling to get out. Pain for mom too. Then I remember trying to understand what I was, and losing my learning techniques. I was 9 months old.

Jordan, age 16: My earliest memories are of time spent with my spirit friends Gutton, Stosh, Tim, Mandy, and a man called Goofball.

Karly, age 23: I remember when I was about 8 months old being fascinated with my hand. I couldn't do much with my hands that was intentional, but I could move them and play with the light through my fingers. I couldn't stop doing it.

Link, age 47: Earth was not formed for my earliest memory. This lifetime, I remember being born. The room was too bright, too loud, too, too great a change, and painful.

Mark, age 40: In the birthing room with bright lights and people in white clothes. A man said, "A really big boy." I weighed 10 pounds.

Michael, age 17: I remember my birth. I remember before birth, too.

Mora, age 36: In my crib watching shadows and feeling the energy produced behind those shadows.

Robert, age 7: I remember being born.

Ryland, age 14: It's like I was dropped into this body. I remember getting out of my crib and walking down the stairs and talking to mom and dad. I have no recall of learning how to talk or walk.

Question 2: Have you always had an understanding of your place in the world?

Angie Carlotta, age 38: No, not completely. I knew I was special, but I didn't know how or why. I felt I did not belong and was put into the wrong family. I would tell that story to my younger sister and imagine how I ended up here.

Anne-Laure: Yes and no. Yes in that I always deeply sensed, but no as I acted so much on "automatic pilot." I did not know who I was.

Ann Marie, age 48: Yes, I have, but I don't think any others believe in or notice my place in the world.

Bill, age 63: Yes. I have always felt that it was my place to help other people, and to share love. Nothing has been more important.

Greg, age 16: Yes, but that place has changed.

James: Yes, but I don't like doing all these weird behaviors. I know I am different and since I was pinned with this frustrating, asinine disability I have issues of anxiety, anger resentment, and deep sadness. I try not to let it overtake me but it is the nature of the beast.

Jordan: I wanted to experience being in this world.

Karly: I began to see that there was a purpose for my life when I was about 10 years old. It began in small ways, but that was around the time that we discovered Facilitated Communication. It gave me the possibility of communicating...I couldn't figure out why I could communicate if there wasn't a reason for it in this world. I am one of the few women with my disorder [Rett's] who can communicate, so it was a strange and unusual event when we discovered it was possible for me to share my inside life through FC. It slowly became possible for me to do other things as well, like composing music, and writing my memoirs, and painting. It changed my life.

Laughing Eagle, age 64: Yes, but I've never understood what anyone else's place is...except in terms of their relationship to me.

Len, age 31: I have faith that all people have a divine purpose that is equal in dignity.

Link: Yes, indeed. Before this incarnation I chose to be born with a disability. I wanted/needed to experience being dependant on others to live. In my other lifetimes I have ruled, led, and taught others, and to some degree I continue to teach in this lifetime; but primarily in this lifetime I am the student.

Maria, age 45: Knew I had to be here, but did not know why (and frankly didn't like at all).

Mark: No, not until I realized I was different than others around me. I was 2 and couldn't express my thoughts, feelings, or wants by speech. Then I internalized and tuned out my surroundings. Not until I was given some sign language did I try to express myself. My family always loved me and accepted me so life was bearable. When I was 25 I was introduced to FC and found my life. I am now telling everyone about my abilities. Not everyone believes in me but those that don't are not important and miss getting to know the funny, smart man I am.

Michael: Not mine, God's. To trust Him is to know I am as I should be.

Ryland: No, not until I met Bill.

Tyler, age 13: Not always, but I do.

Question 3: Have you sensed a divine presence (such as God) close to you? If so, has it been consistent throughout your life?

Angie Carlotta: Absolutely. I will never forget this night as long as I live. I was young, less than 10 years, but I am not sure of the exact age; I was awoken at night and sat up in my bed. By the doorway I observed four bodies of light. They were "talking" to each other. There were no wings or clothes on them; they did not look like ghosts or past people, they were just that—light in the form of bodies with faces. As I was looking on in disbelief, they stopped conversation and one turned her head and looked at me. I do not know the sex but that is what I felt, and there were males too. I couldn't believe what I was seeing and I checked myself to make sure I was awake and I was! I then ducked my head under the blanket and peeked out. I watched as one walked toward my sister's bed and then I saw one come up to mine. I threw my blanket on top my head and stayed under it awake for a long time. My sister never saw anything and no one ever believed me. After that day, I just knew where I belonged, and I prayed and begged my God to take me back.

Ann Marie: Yes, I remember sensing it around age 3, and it has stayed consistent.

Fred: Divine presence is not just close it is always part of my being. It is like this in all my lives.

Gary, age 49: Hard question to answer. I would pray, at 4, for rain and it would. I do feel God is in my life but not every moment of my life.

George: Yes! My grandmother was with me till I was 8 years old; she looked after me lots of the time. Now she is with me in spirit. I also see lots of people in my mind and I keep thinking of them so much; then I actually feel them, touch them, and talk to them clearly and personally in real life. When I tell others the news, they do not believe me, and they think I make it up. They think it's wacky and unreal.

This newly discovered planet—Gliese 581 c—I think is the planet I so called Nevertah from way back. Gliese 581 c is the planet that supports a possibility of life, so does Nevertah. I keep thinking of Nevertah so much that it is real. I have always said that I am originally from the planet Nevertah, which is from a bigger sun from ours. So, Nevertah is finally discovered. Yeah! I have lots of experiences from Nevertah in my past life.

I also believe I have healing powers in my hands. I have often given healing to my mum. These powers come from God.

Greg: No.

Izzy: Yes, God helps me always, in all aspects of my life.

James: I asked God to come into my heart when I was 4 years old. Yes, I know He is always there. Five times I have felt God take over my hate for myself. I know He loves me. I love Him too.

Jordan: Absolutely, my entire life I could feel and hear God speaking directly to me.

Karly: I have always been aware of God. In my early childhood I didn't hear directly from God, but as I got older it became very personal, like the closest of friends. I talk with God about everything now. It is very intimate because He knows everything about me and He helps me find ways to not only improve my life, but to help others who are open to it. I cannot imagine life without my direct connection to God. It is not an easy thing to live with such involved disability, but with the divine presence of God with me, it is a wonderful life, even when it's difficult.

Kyle, age 7: Yes, since I was a baby. He has been a shield of good, so no bad could get me. I don't hear Him as loudly as I used to but (Archangel) Michael is always here.

Laughing Eagle: I've always felt that something/someone unseen was watching me. For many years I thought I was surrounded by a group of angels who were betting over whether I'd make the right choice in any given situation. I still feel myself surrounded by spirits although I no longer think of them as angels. And they're still watching me—but to learn and, yes, be entertained.

Len: I have but I can't say I always do. I have many spiritually dry periods. I have sensed presences both good and evil, and even a mix of both.... I frequently sense a divine presence in plants and animals, particularly dogs. Sometimes I don't realize I'm sensing something until I look back on it.

Link: God is inside me and a part of that divine energy is in all living things.

Maria: Yes, but I would call them my helpers, helping-guiding spirits (like shaman power animals). I don't believe in a creator even though I was raised into the Christian tradition. And yes, I always felt them guiding me.

Mark: There is a spirit that surrounds me with comfort so that could be God. My spirit first came to me when I realized I was different, and is there when I need comfort.

Michael: God is with me always. I talk to Him all the time. In my autistic home He shares His light with me. God does not leave the defenseless alone. Love is what God consists of. We only know one facet of love. There is more to love than imagined by man. Only through suffering is the highest form of love seen. Self over others is the normal hierarchy. For us, suffering yields love of God. God loves us more because of it. God recognizes the committed soul. God rewards us with His continuous presence.

Mora: I always have felt as if I am being watched and guided but the society I live in makes it hard to hear, or sense, rather.

Robert: Yes, He always comes.

Ryland: I can't say that I've sensed God, but, not to go into the theory of physics, I think that I [sensed] my great grandma after she had passed away...I remember feeling a caring warmth. I also have seen dead people and a demon was in my room and attacked me when I was little.

Tyler: When I was little my mom would always ask who my best friend was and I would say God.

Question 4: Does this divine presence guide and inform you? If so, in what ways?

Angie Carlotta: I am at peace and I am learning to listen to my intuition, which is how I feel I am being guided and informed.

Anne-Laure: I believe it is what gave me such survival instincts that allowed me to stay away from certain things and keep going no matter the disapproval I received.

Ann Marie: It guides me without words, with a gentle nudge in a certain direction. It is just a vague feeling. Sometimes I feel like I'm getting a pat on the head, so to speak, as praise for a job well done.

Christopher, age 12: To an extent, I do believe that God is telling me about the future.

Fred: This divine presence gives me my purpose in life. I come to life with information. Then later I dream new directions or read them in words that were given to poets, songwriters, or wise philosophers.

Gary: I use what is called guides. Around normal people I call them the guys upstairs. I have a system that if I hear bells and whistles it is the way to go. I am not always sure what is their will, and what is mine. Sometimes they may see an outcome I can not see. This is where working with guides can be really screwy.

George: These people, or characters, that I see and talk to, motivate me to do well with my school work and my piano, and they help to calm me down when I feel anxious. Sometimes they sit next to me. Sometimes new entities come by me and introduce themselves to me, and I shake their hand. Other people could see them—they are *all real*—but not everyone is ready to see them, which is why they do not appear to others.

Greg: No

Jordan: God tells me what is right and wrong and I follow that lead.

John, age 56: Yes. It informs me of obvious moral dilemmas which most other people seem to miss, and tells me that my eventual death shall be my ticket home provided I manage to hold on to love.

Karly: God and I talk about everything. I ask Him questions about what I should do with my day...God gives me specifics that have not only changed my life, but those around me as well.

Laughing Eagle: I have very vivid dreams that present themselves as identifiable metaphors for events in my life and give me an insight into what I need to do, or how I need to feel, in order to get the best possible result. These dreams have always been accurate. Always.

Len: It does, it draws me to some places and leads me away from others. This doesn't necessarily tell me if where I am is good or bad. Sometimes I can sense a cold feeling about a place or situation not because it's inherently bad but because it's not the place for me at the present moment. Many times I am not guided or informed because I'm not paying attention, my biases are in the way, or I don't process what I'm sensing until it's too late.

Maria: Thoughts pop into my mind which are too strange to be of my origin. Very often dreams which I feel are important (not the usual rubbish). Combination of things I find in nature, strange thoughts and dreams. Quite interesting, and I always felt I'm not lunatic but always knew. I cannot talk about it without sounding lunatic. But then, I don't have a problem with not talking!

Michael: God is there. It is enough just to sense His presence. To ask is to receive an answer, but He answers you, too. Only sometimes the answer is no, and sometimes the answer is later, and sometimes it is in a whisper you do not seem to hear. Most often the answer is "I am here with you. Be not afraid."

Question 5: Do you have insights into human civilization? If so, in what ways?

Angie Carlotta: Many of us like me see the world so different than most, but I am still learning and cannot fully answer this.

Anne-Laure: Autism may or may not have increased, but what increased are the causes for it—artificial this and that—as I believe autism is a reaction to a messed-up environment; of course it shows less in a more natural environment, since then one (like me) is less likely to be in pain.

Bill: I believe civilization is evolving toward the "truth," very slowly, as to be unobserved by the mind but available to the spirit.

Fred: Humans are forever God's children. He gave us life and a planet to be on. Humans were to be His reason to keep this spaceball around. But man disgraces His creation so He is sending tender souls like me to give people reasons to change their ways.

Gary: Because of my autism I was not given the social instincts a normal person has. I feel that it is just a trade off. I only have room for so many talents and sometimes something has to be sacrificed to make room for other gifts. So I have to use my abilities as a clairvoyant and my great analytical abilities to understand how humans work and their motivations.

George: Humans have to understand the history of the universe and evolution. It is not every day that we can create life out of something inanimate. How did humans become themselves and be who they are now? And from understanding where we are now, we can look into, and help, the future. We could possibly become the perfect life forms, physically and spiritually.

Greg: Yeah, I could specify the insights: people think in terms of attributes and things. They simplify large numbers of things by putting those things into a group and assigning the group attributes, then thinking of individuals in that group by how they differ from the group as a whole. I guess that is more human thinking, but how we think guides our civilization—mostly tribalism. People consider themselves members of many groups, and tend to think ill of people outside said groups. No matter how hard a big country tries, it can't beat an entrenched rebellion—it can, however, defeat itself.

Izzy: People can be very mean, very judgmental. They don't understand other people if they haven't "walked in their shoes."

Jordan: I think so it going to be a long time before the end is near.

Len: I see human nature as inherently good, but fallen and influenced by our egos. I don't believe the ego is the cause of all suffering but of most suffering and everybody has it. I don't like to see people as all bad or all good since we continue to have free will and struggle with good and evil until the moment of death. I see a lot of polarization and ego-driven, us-versus-them thinking. This is affecting politics, world religions, making it hard for people to put biases aside, and is dividing society.

Karly: I see how people's actions affect the lives of others as well as their own.

Laughing Eagle: I have a vision of the development of human civilization and our various religious and philosophical beliefs. The message is clear: Regardless of the words we use to describe anything that's "supernatural," what they're based on is the same. Different people and societies are merely interpreting them differently based on their own backgrounds.

Mark: Yes, we are being tested with all kinds of problems and how we handle them will determine the fate of the world. I know that there are more difficult times ahead, but not what they are to be. I have hope that my spirit will protect all those important around me, and that everyone has a spirit protector.

Mora: Yes we are going to evolve into ways currently unimaginable and unthinkable by today's standards, emotionally or biologically.

Nick, age 32: The increase of technology has created conditions on earth that are probably similar to that of the non-material realm. On the astral plane, telepathy is the language of the sprit. One can contact anyone else and get an instant reply. On our dense earth plane, the internet, cell phones, and other technological advances have created the conditions that are beginning to mimic the lighter and more flexible conditions of our "true home." I think human beings are beginning to collectively realize this. The world is shrinking and with each succeeding generation, we are beginning to realize that we are all a part of each other. We rise or fall...sink or swim together. Our very survival depends on this realization.

Richie, age 13: Yes, I see when people will pass away.

Ryland: I don't but wish I did.

Tyler: Yes, when I see auras. I can tell how people are feeling at the time. If they are feeling good, they will have a really light color and if they are mad, angry, or sad it will be dark.

Question 6: Do you have insights into the future of our civilization? If so, in what ways?

Angie Carlotta: I did, unfortunately, I can't remember all of what I know, and I hope it comes back to me. We are not what we were taught to believe we are. There is so much more knowledge out there but many are too stubborn to see and believe.

Anne-Laure: The only way to make the world sustainable is to share our different perspectives; we are all in it together and can learn from one another.

Christopher: Kind of, but not about everybody. I have random thoughts throughout the day and dreams about different things at night. I feel like there are both good and bad things around us and things that may happen to people.

Gary: I have seen a possible future for about 20 years. It appears to happen when I am in my mid-50s. If it is true, the human race is in trouble.

George: Humans tend to do what they feel is comfortable. They would destroy anything to make themselves comfortable on Earth. They believe they are the bosses of the Earth. But they forget that before the human race, there were other living life forms which were greater and more intelligent than humans. There would be less natural resources, more artificially happy people, and less happy other-living things if humans continue to be careless about the world. It will be an ideal world if humans were naturally happy and used their energies well.

Izzy: Only God knows exactly what the future will hold.

Jordan: I can't foresee destruction; I see peace.

Len: I see the recession ending gradually but it may take longer for people to realize it. I believe there will be a lot of creative ideas coming out of this. I see an informal barter system developing based on reciprocal relationships. I see people finding ways to become better informed and looking for ways to increase self-sufficiency, complementary medicine, nutrition, and herbs will be one example. Another would be growing our own food, even in urban settings. I see people becoming more thrifty and frugal with money and time by realizing how much resources we waste. I see technology increasing at a rapid pace and having both pros and cons. I see the Internet advancing and more people working from home as well as getting educated from home. I see more movement of people around the world and around the country causing more exposure to new ideas, and fusions between cultures causing fear and anxiety in some, but leading to more tolerance. I see the polemics in both religions and politics to continue and possibly worsen before people realize how irrational they are. I see a coming together of eastern and western ideas in religion and especially Christianity with the west becoming less legalistic in theology. I see Eastern Christianity (Orthodox, Assyrians) becoming more noticed and mysticism (not necessarily of the New Age variety) becoming more accepted in the West. I believe there will be climate change, not all of it caused by man, but not enough to panic over. I feel it may cause some problems and require some adaptations, but I feel it can also have a silver lining. (That's not to say we shouldn't do our part to respect the planet.) I also see a movement away from big cities and some rural areas and moving more toward mid-sized and small cities.

Maria: If I look at what this civilization is doing to Mother Earth, how they spoil their own base they thrive on, I am sure this "civilization" will vanish—sooner than later. And the Earth will start a new try.

Mark: We are in deep trouble with so much greed and no morals. We need to stop thinking about ourselves and focus on the needs of others.

Michael: I know things about the future through what I know about my future. I know euthanasia is coming, the last holocaust. God is not going to let the world continue as it is. Shortages will make life a cheap commodity. Our disabled will be the first dispensables. Only it is best others not know what they are capable of, I think. I will not answer until God says it is time. God is in control so I do not fear the failures of man. God is with a plan. Some may hinge on our choices. God knows those choices already. God accounted for them long ago.

Nick: I believe with each succeeding generation, we are going to find more and more world unity. Human beings yearn for it. We yearn to create Heaven on earth. It is in our spiritual DNA for this to be the case. How could it not be? We were all one at the time of the big bang.

So what's stopping us from achieving this goal? In our material world, there are a finite number of resources that human beings compete for. In our spiritual home, there are no such things as resources. Such is the task of our lives. To collectively create a similar environment on earth that mimics our true home, under more challenging conditions than that of our true home. This is the reason we chose to undertake lives on this planet. It is the reason that the big bang happened; collectively, the universe (God) knew that every part of itself had to "experience" itself in order for God to truly know Him/Herself. So as individual fragments of God, each of us chose to come to earth for the exact same reason. To experience ourselves as an extension of God and accelerate each of our soul's development so that one day, we can and will all ultimately to the Godhead. Once we have done our part to create paradise on this plane, we will be ready to eventually merge with it directly. As above, so below. If you need proof of what I am saying, just look at fractals: the micro mimics the macro.

Richie: Yes, I see an honest and loving world ahead filled with music and genuine caring of one another.

Tyler: Yes, I always used to draw the solar system. I would draw the planets in alignment with a bunch of meteors hitting the earth. I think this is something that will happen, because what I saw seemed so real. It was like X-Box 360 quality of graphics, images that just popped in my head. I also had a dream about a plane blowing up in the sky a couple nights before 9/11.

Question 7: Are you fearful or optimistic about your insights?

Bill: Optimistic. We have nothing to fear.

Christopher: They are both good and bad insights, mostly it doesn't bother me, but a few things I see aren't good. For instance, sometimes I can foresee the end of the world and it will happen through a gigantic chain of natural disasters, earthquakes on a scale of greater than 9.5, gigantic tsunamis, tornados, twisters, and hurricanes beyond anything we could count.

James: I am sad that people cannot see God like I can. I am sad that I cannot let them know because of my autism. Some people believe me because they know that there is nothing too difficult for God. Others, who say they are Christians, only see me with the doubt of worldly ways.

Jordan: Optimistic.

George: I think things on Earth will be okay only if humans continue to progress in the work of humanity, for the sake of humans and for animals, plants, and other life.

Izzy: Optimistic.

Karly: I rarely am fearful about them, because it's not my purpose to make others change, but rather to give insights. Those insights come from God, He knows the person and their situation, I don't. I just pass on the message. I feel optimistic if the person hears and respects the message that was given to me for them. It is rarely a hopeless one, usually God gives me a message that gives them guidance or direction and opens their hearts. It gives them joy. This world is made up of people. Each one has their own story and God knows each one. I am used to give a few individuals a direct message.

Len: I'm optimistic, but that doesn't mean I don't see potential problems. I do understand that when problems get solved, new ones come to take their place. For example, a cure for a disease is found and new ones take their place. And, just in the way in which viruses mutate and become resistant to drugs, the human ego in its many faces and forms will always have a new trick up its sleeve. I feel it's a cycle that continues as we become more spiritually mature up until the moment we are called home. The most important reason to be optimistic about is the afterlife, which we will always have the free will to accept or reject, and therefore the only things we would have to fear are pride and despair.

Maria: Neither. Things will happen as they will. Fear or optimism won't change anything, so it is of no use to be fearful. And I cannot be optimistic. How could you if you have a clear look at the world?

Mora: Optimistic but not for this millennia.

Nick: I am optimistic about my insights.

Ryland: I don't feel that I have any.

Tyler: I'm more fearful because if I was right about 9/11, I must be right about the asteroids and meteors.

Question 8: Do you believe your insights will manifest or are they only forecasts?

Anne-Laure: I don't know, though there are more and more people on the autism spectrum and they share a little bit at a time about their world.

Gary: They are only forecasts. Things can change.

Jordan: Peace will manifest.

Karly: It's not up to me if they manifest. For me, the messages I get for individuals are real and powerful. If they listen, it will change them but it's not up to me. They choose their futures, not me. I am just the messenger. There are times when my messages don't take place, like I was directed, but it is usually because of something out of any of our controls. It's often very accurate, more often than not.

Len: I feel all things can be changed by the right choices and by prayer. Some things such as natural disasters cannot always be changed, but they can still lead to a greater good though that greater good won't always be realized in this life.

Link: Quite a silly question. The past reflects the present and the future is never set. I can only say I hope mankind continues to try to remember the true nature of our beings.

Maria: If we won't change now our behavior toward our fellow beings (plants, animals, humans), it will be too late for a change. No Gods or spiritual beings (or whatever you might call them) are helping anyone who spoils their gifts. Insofar this might be only a forecast but it will manifest, the less we care for our world.

Mark: Like mom, I am a Pollyanna. So, yes, I think we can overcome this, but it will take time.

Nick: I believe they will manifest when human beings can look at another person, an animal, or even a blade of grass, and see themselves as being a part of whatever it is they are looking at. When we value the earth and the universe as much as we do ourselves, I believe these insights will manifest.

Tyler: Yes, I believe they will manifest.

Question 9: What can we do to guide and inform others (including non-believers) about such insights?

Anne-Laure: As for myself, I try to write about it. I believe that informing is important, and whether non-believers like it or not does not matter so much in the big picture as autism is here, though it makes it hard to share.

Ann Marie: There is probably nothing we can do to inform or guide non-believers since they are in the dark and unable to listen. These people will only come out of the dark and wake up if they encounter enough pain in their ignorance. So, to guide we can only stop enabling them to live in denial (darkness), and stop supporting or encouraging their denial, but this is usually difficult.

Bill: Talk about them, and invite inquiry into one's own self; to see who we truly are. This must be done with love.

Gary: I do not believe we should live in the future. We should live in the present. When I work with others my goal is to work with them to obtain their highest potential. To worry about the future or some off-shoot will take away from their work in this lifetime.

George: Lots of people are paranoid and ignorant, and will not let themselves see. There are clouds in their faces blocking their view from believing the insights. We have to try to motivate them and be their friends. Slowly, they will come around when they do nice things. Teach them by example.

Greg: I happen to be a non-believer myself (is Contrarianisim a religion?), so I think I might have an easier time convincing people then, say, your average street-corner prophet. That said, my insights are a combination of cold-reading style covering of all of my bases, and observation-based predictions. If you sum up all of my insights, however, there is not much action that the average person would need to take—I'm not saying that people should change, or that they would benefit much from changing. I mean, high-fructose corn syrup is not much different from sucrose! People aren't much different from chimps!

Izzy: First, they must believe in God, have faith, and put their faith in Him. We have to try to teach others that everyone has special talent.

Karly: I am a Christian. There are many Christians who believe they know what God is like, but their experience of God is very different than mine. However, there are some who are so eager to hear a message from God that they are thrilled. God knows who they are. I don't seek them out, He sends them to me. If all people were open, this world would be an incredible place because God can guide each person....We would be fulfilled, and we would be there for others. We would not be isolated and lonely.

Len: Persuade and have patience, never force. Never be patronizing and always let people save face when they discover their mistakes. Humility in us is essential since it is not possible to serve a greater good and serve our egos at the same time. Teach by example. Don't label people, condemn them, and then expect them to embrace your ideas. Make sure all ideas pursued are for the greater good of all human beings, and at the expense of not one soul or the idea will only backfire.

Link: Easier said than done. We each can send energy and light to each other, but each individual must get more open and remember.

Maria: Nothing. If people don't care for the gifts that are offered to them no one can change their minds. Remember: free will.

Nick: Do not insist that people believe in "God" for humanity to achieve world unity. Pantheism and Buddhism is just as spiritual as Orthodox Judaism or Roman Catholicism. Help others to see that all spiritual paths lead to the same place, which is our collective destiny. Encourage other autistics to speak their minds, regardless of what they believe.

Tyler: Just putting stories like this in the book you're writing is a good start.

Question 10: What would you wish for the average reader to understand about what you've shared?

Angie Carlotta: Open your mind—we all have a purpose here, even those who you do not think are offering us something; often they are smarter than you.

Anne-Laure: That environmental improvements are a necessity if human civilization is to survive. That "herding" of people in large groups is more detrimental to our civilization that we know. That autism is a reaction to an artificial environment. That we are all in it together.

Ann Marie: I believe that we are all spiritual beings having a temporary physical experience here on earth, but only some people recognize or acknowledge their own or another's spirituality. Anyone reading these comments I've made needs to look at them from a spiritual perspective, lest they think I am crazy, a zealot, or an idiot.

Bill: That life is an illusion. That we are so much more than we perceive. We are not "beings" as in a "thing," but "being" itself. We are love itself.

Christopher: Natural disasters are naturally occurring and enough are about to happen that human civilization might end. There's no technology available now to stop it, but maybe in the future the technology will be available.

Fred: I wish the average reader understands that we need to treat Earth much better than we did during the last century.

Gary: I know older autistic people who are not spiritual because they hid their talents so as to fit in. These people had to sacrifice their talents so as to be able to fit into society. I have never blended in completely and nor have I stayed in a field that would be successful so life has been hell. My stepson is definitely autistic. He can not fit in completely, but he is learning the skills needed to fit in as best as possible. He is also spiritual, but I do not talk with him about being clairvoyant. He has seen me do the spiritual work but I am going to let him come to his own conclusions.

Greg: Just because I'm on the spectrum does not mean that God can talk to me! Furthermore, he actually has a pretty bad record when it comes to predictions, so I'm not sure I'd take it at face value anyhow. There is not much you can do with my predictions other then hedge your bets about how long you'll live, and don't delay things that will make you happy because you never know when we'll all get vaporized without warning.

Izzy: That my faith is strong, to never question God. You must believe; I always will.

James: I want them to know that I am as much a gift from God as they are. He looks at our hearts, not our outside.

Jordan: Believe in a power greater than you, listen to your minds and thoughts, and follow them—this is God.

Karly: I want to have people open their minds and hearts. Those of us who are living with what appears to be great challenges are often very spiritual and connected to God. If they knew what was in our lives and hearts that is not visible, they would be eager to get to know us. We have insights that are not common or ordinary. We need more patience from people. We need them to slow down and listen with their hearts.

Kyle: Mother Nature gets mad at people that litter trash and plastic and do not do their part so she finds the ones who care and she gets them to fix things. God told me, or maybe it was (Archangel) Michael, I think it was Michael.

Laughing Eagle: I think it's important to understand that what most of us are raised to believe is the "real" world is only one form that reality takes. If we're open enough we can experience many more realities. Often simultaneously.

Len: That although I have a lot to say I, first, don't claim to be always right; and second, that while I reject rigid dichotomies and blind ideology, my intention is not to write my own ideology, philosophy, or start my own religion. I have heard an expression that when people try to organize "truth" it becomes a lie. I feel this is true in most cases and it may have something to do with the ego. Once people label something they like they begin to identify with it, and a new us-and-them develops. A non-ideology then becomes an ideology. I can't say I'm against organized religion as I am Roman Catholic, but I do reject us-versus-them thinking. I do believe in absolute truth, but not in excess abstraction or oversimplifying real life. Finally, that I may be autistic and autistic people are understood to be literal and concrete thinking, it does not mean that they are not capable of mystical understandings and spiritual insights. It's a paradox, but autism is a paradoxical condition.

Maria: Please honor every life. This planet is a beautiful jewel in the black cold nothing. We should take responsibility for our actions or this beautiful gift will be lost to us forever. Don't fool yourself: Earth does not need us but we need the Earth.

Mark: Have open minds about what you don't understand. Believe that just because we are different we have valid thoughts and can be helpful in solving problems. Be sure to accept us as real people and respect our talents. It is hard to do because we can look different and sometimes act weird. But give us a chance to prove our worth.

Michael: My relationship with God.

Mora: The vast majority of people are blind; the "fully" able are actually the ones with the disability.

Nick: It can sometimes be easy to be cynical in a place where tragedies are as common as sipping a cup of coffee. Yet I would suggest that whatever happens here (on earth) is merely to present us with a series of tests to further our spiritual development. When we realize the impermanence of our lives creates an illusory drama that traps us, we can free up that trapped energy to create a better world for all. As the great Shakespeare so accurately observed, "All the world is a stage." Let's have a happy ending!

Reinhold, age 19: I don't need to express my thoughts into language for myself, so I don't write or speak a lot. My mind is similar to the Taoistic and Buddhistic ideals; I think very instinctively and impulsively.

Richie: That autistic people are gifted, not disabled.

Ryland: That I am not making this stuff up. I am seriously not lying. Demons and ghosts are real. Maybe it's a conditional thing; maybe other people can't see them. I just want to be believed.

Tyler: It would be nice if the reader would believe what I'm saying.

With the exception of Mark and Fred, I wish to note that none of the people who completed the survey know one another, although I know a number of them personally (and specifically reached out to them), or, at the least, I have had ongoing contact with their parents or caregivers. I was surprised, intrigued, and validated as I opened my e-mail letterbox to receive their responses. With their answers in hand, my next challenge was to collate the information with some measure of cohesion and draft a summary of my tabulations. Then, I received one last survey returned from a latecomer that would perhaps prove to be among the most compelling and erudite commentaries of all.

Chapter 8

Wally's Wisdom

*"Our task must be to free ourselves...by widening our circle
of compassion to embrace all living creatures and the whole
of nature and its beauty."*
—Albert Einstein

More than anyone, Wally Wojtowicz, Jr., committed grand expanses
of time to answering my spiritual questionnaire—throughout the period
of more than two months and three revisions he deliberated, edited, and
finessed his replies. Wally is now a middle-aged man who was diagnosed
with autism at age 2; about the same time, in hindsight, he had an epiph-
any that, "at a very young age I realized I had a feeling that there was
a power over my reality." By age 9, Wally also had grand-mal epilepsy,
but liberation came at 25 when he learned to type, revealing remarkably
inspired thoughts. In contrast, his mother, Gay, recalled the clinical supposition she and her husband had leveled at them with banal finality, "We
were told Wally didn't understand anything that was said to him, or have
any feelings." Wally developed ALS, or Lou Gehrig's, at age 35, causing
his limbs to become unreliable, such that he is now virtually immobilized.

Wally presently communicates through some supported typing or
by using a laser device in tandem with a computer. His father, Wally,
Sr., explained, "Wally used both the Tobii Eye Gaze computer and
Facilitated Communication while working on this piece. The majority
was typed with FC because it is faster at this point for him than is using
the eye gaze. The eye gaze computer has a camera that tracks Wally's
eyes as he looks at a target (the letter he wants to type) and then after
Wally dwells on the target for a fraction of a second the computer types

the letter that he was looking at." (Anyone intrigued with learning more about Wally and his family may view filmmaker Teo Zagar's video, *Heart Savants*, online at *www.youtube.com*.)

As I began to read Wally's responses I had the unenviable, but necessary, task of deciding how best to excerpt them, to arrange his words and insert them alongside the others. I quickly came to appreciate that Wally hadn't just responded to a poll, he had composed introspective, serious, and thought-provoking *essays* in order to provide us with his most complete and thorough reaction to each question posed.

My reluctant attempt to edit salient snippets of Wally's responses in the general text of this book soon proved futile, and I determined to honor Wally's words by including the full account of his replies here. Nothing is excised, and I am reproducing this valuable information word-for-word so that we may all glimpse the ethereal beauty of Wally's fascinating insights and amazing wisdom—the spiritual fruit that comes from living in meditative silence, and without spoken language, as Wally does.

Question 1: What are your earliest memories of being in the world?

Wally, age 42: I think that what you are asking with this question is, when did you know that you were a being of some sort, or when did you become aware of your self. If my understanding of your question is correct, then my answer will be that I recognized my being, or my self, while still in my mother's womb.

I realized that I was a being when I was in utero. The realization of one's self is the defining rational that is the difference that separates the human from other beings or creations of nature. My point that I want to make is that each being will realize his self when thoughts are formulated and one becomes aware that he produced the thought.

The idea that the human being in utero is not technically a living being is a sad comment on human civilizations worldwide. Yet I watch the emergency medical crews fighting to revive a child that was too underdeveloped at a premature birth by giving it oxygen while in another operating room an unborn baby is killed in an abortion by many of the same team. My autistic mind can not grasp the differences between these two scenarios that make one life more valuable than the other. In my mind, both infants, one born and one unborn, are living beings and deserve to be treated equally. Both should be given an equal chance at life.

I have vivid conscious recollections of the time before my birth. I know that I reasoned, though not with your language, but with my own internal language that I had started to develop when I was first conceived. I built on this internal language all through my life. I am still using this internal language in its expanded form to think with even today. I think in this internal language though I write in yours. Yet, I, too, reason with my internal language after I have first translated your words to mine. In reverse, I must translate my thoughts that are in my internal language into your language before I type.

People who consider themselves to be reasonable will no doubt find it in their mind to be an impossibility that I was able to start to develop my internal language in utero and be aware of this. I know what I say sometimes sounds too far out in the minds of some people, but I tell it like it is. It is of no consequence to me what others think of my thoughts because most other people do not have the very acute senses that I have and have not experienced the world from my perspective. As I am aware of others' thoughts and thus their limitations, I am not deterred in what I can now express.

I want you to know that the idea that life begins at conception is, I feel, true. This simple activation of the soul at the moment of conception is the beginning of life. Though I think that I began life in utero, at conception, others will argue the point. They will say that life begins at birth. Though there is no quick answer to the question of when does life begin, I am convinced in my mind that I was a life at conception. As I am in no way an expert in the field of deciding when life begins, I will defer to those who voice the opposite position to mine if and when they can prove without any doubt that the fertilized human egg, though only one cell, does not contain life and is not truly alive. I understand that all fertilized eggs will not be viable and all will not attain the proper care to develop into live beings that will live full lives. This is in the hands of nature.

The basic reality is that once there is life, there is the potential for thought. The philosopher, Rene Descartes, once said, "I think therefore I am." The rudimentary thinking that I was engaged in before I was born is that of the most basic of ideas that one can have. For example, realizing when the day light and nighttime was; when there were loud and strange noises; when we were moving about; when I eavesdropped on the muffled conversations of others who were in close proximity to my mother; when I was uncomfortable; and realizing that I was about to be born. These examples of what I experienced and what I knowingly reacted to are not peculiar to me as other humans and unborn fetuses of other species experience them also,

The aspect that separates me and probably others like me from other living beings is the presence of a conscious awareness that something was happening, along with the ability to remember. In utero, I did not know what light and darkness were. In utero, I did not know what motion was, nor did I know what sound was. I did know, however, that there was something that I was reacting to even though I only had my rudimentary internal language to inform my self with. With this language, I was only able to explain to my self that something was happening, something different as I experienced one type or another of stimulus, some pleasing and comforting, and some not.

I truly think that the principal of the soul marking the beginning of a human life at conception is a true and accurate statement. There was one other saying in keeping with this topic that I had thought of previously, "Yesterday you were a thought, today, you have thoughts." The thoughts that I had in utero are not as important at this time as is the realization that I had thoughts, therefore I was. Thoughts are only the waves of the universe lapping at the shores of our minds. The waves, though silent in their approach, will let ideas erupt in our minds and flow like a river of searing lava throughout our lives.

Realizing that our thoughts are the activity of our minds, I am ecstatic to tell you that "I am." Realizing "I am" will not the person make, though realizing I am truly a person is for me a true and exciting revelation of my mind. In thinking, the idea that "I was," if thought about, is exciting because I could bring to my consciousness that which I had previously experienced. I could tell my self that I had experienced the precise stimuli previously and identify that which was comfortable and that which would cause me discomfort though I didn't know your terms for these sensations. Thinking without the benefit of a language is only possible if one can think in pictures or in some type of mental image. The point that the reader should take from my answer is that I was aware of various stimuli in utero and have definite and vivid recollections of these stimuli.

Question 2: Have you always had an understanding of your place in the world?

Wally: Each person born will, at some point, question why he exists. I must admit that I had no idea of why I existed. The thought of why I existed never entered my mind until sometime after I was able to communicate with the world that existed outside of my body. This was after I was 25 years old.

Years ago, I thought that I was the thought of the two wills that were inhabiting the individual known as Wally Wojtowicz, Jr. Yet, I was able to think thoughts on my own as the two wills would compete for the control of the little boy Wally. I envisioned my self as an ether spirit with no physical body that you would recognize as Wally, Jr. I considered my self as thought energy that emanated from the two wills. One will was the impulsive autistic will and the other being the contemplative thinking will. These two wills were recognized by me, but one will did not know that the other existed in the same individual.

I, the self, recognized their existence. I was able to witness the two wills trying to simultaneously control the little boy Wally. It was as if I was watching these two wills each playing its part out on a separate stage that was not seen by the other. From my vantage point, I could experience both performers trying to control Wally. I was not able to intervene to help Wally at the time, but would try to redirect him toward the contemplative will's influence when ever possible. It wasn't until I was able to communicate, starting at age 25, that I realized that I was the sum total of both wills. I finally realized that I, the ether spirit, was a real, living, and thinking person who was known to others as "Little Wally" or "Baby Wally." I knew this individual intimately and now would think that I wanted to take control of the boy Wally.

The reality of looking at two wills to deal with was without a doubt overwhelming at times, but I knew that I had to connect the reality of my life to that of the master plan for my place or my involvement in the world. I now know that my purpose in the "big picture" is to be a bridge that will connect the world of the nonverbal autistic people to the world and reality of those who consider themselves to be "normal."

One person's thinking often is not without bias, making it difficult for him to take into consideration the rest of mankind's wisdom. I never thought that upon my principals would rest the answer to this second question. Each thinking person is thought to know that he, as a human being, if questioned about his place in the world's plan on any occasion, would tell you that he was without any clue to his purpose in the world other than repeating the generation of the species. Often, our place or our job in the "grand plan" is not initially known by the individual. However, given enough time, the individual, if at all aware, will figure out his place or purpose in the world.

Years back, before I could communicate, the notion of what exactly was my purpose in life almost consumed my being. I thought at one time that I easily existed to be the mediator between the two wills that inhabited the boy Wally. Reality for me at that time did not indicate that I could be a contributing member of our society. I was not encouraged by society to strive for anything other than a place in the back row of life. Thoughts of rocking and bobbing, and of stimming, for hours on end in a group home somewhere were reinforced in my mind each day while I confronted the staff at the various day programs I attended. Rather than being groomed to be a contributor to society, I was in essence being groomed to be a burden on society. I actually was thinking that the people I was exposed to wanted me to be the perfect inmate in one of the programs for adults. Some people's ideas of my potential in the "grand plan" were based on an outdated paradigm where the nonverbal autistic was placed in rank just below that of a dog. This was especially true of those people charged with my early education some 36 or 38 years ago.

Looking back on my life, I know that I was clueless as to my place in the world. This would last until I started to learn to communicate with the outside world using Facilitated Communication at the age of 25. It was easy to escape into "my world" of autism rather than face the realities of the real world that existed outside of my body, "your world." Once I learned to communicate, I was able to realize a perspective on my life that I found at the same time to be both frightening as well as intriguing. I'm still frightened at times by what I sense as total chaos in the world that exists just outside of my body. However, my ever-present need to explore and examine the reality I now accept as "our world," the world that I share with you, is what is driving me to find my place in this world. Justice, equality, and reasonable quality of life are, in my mind, the goals that I now seek for my self and for those who have no voice. I now understand my place in the world; to be a link between the nonverbal autistic people and those who consider themselves to be "normal." Reaching this conclusion, I am convinced, is the point in my life where I'll be the happiest and most fulfilled.

When I perceived my self, I did not realize that I was an individual person made up of the two wills plus the intellect, or the self. I always thought that the individual wills as I perceived them in my mind were separate and distinct beings from each other and from my self. In other words, I recognized three complete individuals: the impulsive autistic will; the contemplative will; and the ether spirit self. I represented these three individuals to my mind to save confusing them with the person of Little Wally; the either spirit that understands, the impulsive autistic will that is fighting the contemplative will for control of Wally, the sophisticated contemplative will that understands that I am in charge of Wally. These three "individuals" that I recognize are constituents of little Wally's person.

Each of my wills pleases the boy, Wally, at different times. The autistic will was socially inept thus raising the ire of those who were working with the little boy. The autistic will when in control of the little boy took every opportunity to discourage Wally from considering his place in the grand scheme of life. Rather, the autistic will taught Wally that he was the center of the universe and everyone and everything around him was there for his pleasure i.e., Wally was the unmistakable ruler of his realm even though it was an autistic realm. Being the center of his universe, the autistic Wally did not consider that in his world there was any need to think of other people who were orbiting him like planets revolving around the sun nor did he consider his place in the grand plan other than being the center. This was to change when the contemplative will was in control.

The two wills were constantly fighting for control of the boy Wally. This battle was going on since Wally was in utero. Yet, there were specks of the contemplative will's influence that would shine through the blackness that the autistic will would drape the little boy with. Every now and then, when Wally was a youngster, the contemplative will's influence would be very apparent to those who knew Wally as well as to his self. These tiny shimmers of normalcy gave hope to Wally's family and to his self. Though these expressions of normalcy were overlooked by all but the most astute observers, Wally's life had already in some minds been regarded as a useless waste.

In winning, the contemplative will would expose the reality of the world to Wally even if only for brief peeks which were enough to entice him to seek more and more. It was during these brief encounters with reality that Wally's self thought of his place in the world that he was slowly becoming a part of. It was during these brief interludes of reality that Wally's self reached the conclusion that his place in the world would be as a link or a bridge between the nonverbal autistic world and the reality that he craved and wanted now to be a part of. The reality was realized over many years, during which time my contemplative will was strengthened by my self or my intellect which watched the two wills struggle for control. I understand my place in the world is unique, though quietly, I much prefer to be involved with my work of being the link or bridge in the privacy of my mind which extends to my written thoughts.

Let your hopes taste your dreams so that they will treat your soul—by Wally Wojtowicz, Jr.

Question 3: Have you sensed a divine presence (such as God) close to you? If so, has it been consistent throughout your life?

Wally: Questions about the "power" that I experience in my life, as one who is not supposed to have the rational to experience any more than an amoeba does, have always intrigued me. I am truly respectful of the amoeba. I respect them because of who, or what, created them. I truly am impressed by the amoeba's complexities even though it is one cell. I think that I could not match, in a thousand lifetimes of trying, the beauty of simplicity and complexity that is embodied in each one of these living creatures. To examine the amoeba is to examine that expression of our own lives and to interpret what we have gleaned from this examination in terms of who or what power made both.

Thinking as to who or what power created the beautiful tiny amoeba will only quantify for me that man did not do it. Maybe thousands of years hence, man might be able to create a creature that might resemble an amoeba. However, will man have advanced enough to give life to their creation? I think not. Man, a thousand years from now, might have the ability to transplant life from something that is living to one of his creations, but I think that man will not easily achieve the ability to create life in any form that we now know. You realize the beauty of the amoeba if you think of the power that created it. Yet, in thoughts about this creator we notice that our mental representation of this power is in the likeness of ourselves. I often wonder, realizing I often speculate about the impossible, if the one-celled amoeba is aware of its creator as I am aware of mine.

I truly believe that there is some power that exists that is greater than man. You can call this power God, or refer to it by some other name. Thoughts of this power have always been present in my mind. I have not had any physical confirmation of this power such as a sighting, or the sensation of a strange pressure or aroma that might indicate something out of the ordinary. I only perceive this power as being always present in my mind. I recognized the presence of this power as far back as I can remember, which for me extends to my existence in utero.

Thoughts of this power have been with me all of my life. You must remember that I believe that life begins for a new human being at conception. Thoughts about this power being God have been in my consciousness since my baptism into the Catholic Church. Teachings of the Church helped me put into words and thoughts the personification of the presence that I always welcomed and recognized.

I think that I feel the presence of the power that I now refer to as God in the reality of my life. Thinking back to the time before I could consistently reason clearly, which is the period of my life before I could communicate with the world that surrounds me, each new discovery that I made only made me wonder who was responsible for that which I became aware of. I knew somehow that something or someone was responsible for the world that I was experiencing outside of my mind. This question haunted me, yet I somehow knew the answer to the question of who, or what, made everything that I experienced. I didn't have a name or term for this power, but I knew that it existed.

The realization for me that God was the ever-present power was made clear to me as I thought about the world that I experienced. Yet, before I could communicate with "your world," I told myself that I was responsible for everything that I sensed. However, I knew, deep in my mind, that I was not the real creator of all that I experienced. The presence that I was aware of that I now call God simply was of no surprise to me. The presence of this power in my life was instrumental in my ability to cope with my life. This power not only helped me rationalize the worlds that I was experiencing, but it also kept me from the abyss of insanity by being the "glue" that held my fragile world together and gave substance to my life.

Each one of the various creations that I was aware of could perhaps be the product of evolution, which I don't question because there has to be some power that guides this process. I prefer to think of this guiding power as God. To be aware of God is the power that will unite the civilizations of the world. I understand that our universal conceptualization of God will probably not be embraced by all people, but there will be consensus, at least, that there is some power greater than man.

Question 4: Does this divine presence guide and inform you? If so, in what ways?

Wally: I think what you are asking with this question is whether or not I have experienced any indications from God as direct answers to my petitions for specifics that one might ask for from one more powerful than himself. I must answer no to this question. In years past, I thought that God was going to listen to my every request with the interest of a parent when confronted with his child's Christmas list and deliver that which the child asked for. I thought that I could receive what I petitioned for by praying perfectly with prayers that I had become familiar with in church services or that I had learned in Sunday school.

I asked, I prayed, I asked some more, and I prayed harder than I ever did. I recited prayer after prayer, over and over, in an attempt to build up my "prayer savings account." I figured that if my "prayer savings account" got large enough, God would surely listen to my requests and couldn't possibly ignore delivering the "goods." When this approach produced no results I threatened to become an atheist or an agnostic. I did neither nor did I renounce my faith when my prayers produced no physical results. I didn't pray for a bike or some other toy, nor did I pray for a pony. I thought that other children would want these things. Thoughts of material items were never on my list that I was petitioning for. I had only asked to be cured of my autism. To me, this was a reasonable request when considering my circumstances.

I also thought the world would stop revolving around the sun if I wasn't cured of my autism. The world is doing fine with its orbiting of the sun. I am, without a doubt, still autistic, but I am withering slowly away as I now have ALS. This disease is, I know, my reward for all of my praying to God for a cure for my autism. The only problem I now have is that I can't walk or use my arms or hands. I am totally paralyzed from the ALS. The good news is that I am now as close to being "normal" as I ever will be; this is what I prayed so hard for. I can sit at a table with family or friends and not once grab another's pork chop or steak from their plates as I once did. I am now very neat when I eat or drink. Every now and then, though, I do spill a few drops of food or drink from my feeding tube, but this is nothing when compared to the messes I made when I fed myself or when I would charge across the table with a full body dive to retrieve some epicurean delight from another's plate or in some instances from another's hand. I am now able to enjoy the company of other people without running away from them. I put my trust in my God to make me as "normal" as possible and He listened and He delivered. I thank God for these rewards.

Each time that I am about to turn my back on the universal principals of our Catholic faith, years of effort that were poured into my religious education flash before me. This, to me, is the unrelenting work of my God tapping me on the head to let me know that He is watching over me all of the time and that He is in my life. You must realize the importance of the awareness that shadows your thoughts that the power or God is in your soul. The awareness of a higher power has expressed itself over the years many times to me. I pray more now because I am more aware of my God's presence in my life. As I mentioned previously, I always knew that there was something bigger than man that had an influence on all that there is or was or will be. This power, or God, reminds me to think before I act; informs me of the power of prayer; reminds me that I, too, will be in His presence forever. Each time I satisfy my urges to do something I know is wrong, I am reminded of God's presence in my life. These reminders not only make me aware that I am not alone on my journey but remind me that I will some day find total peace in God's presence. I might get that tap on the head, or find that I am regretful after committing some infraction of His law, or I might be reminded of my deviation from God's wisdom by the sharp words from one of my family or friends. In any event, I take these reminders as signs that I am in the presence of something that is not only real, but is guiding me every step of my journey with pure love and compassion.

I can't say that I have ever received any direct instructions from God to do or not do something. I haven't received any direct intervention when I was about to make an error of some type. Nor was I told that I had just erred. I find that I was given the intellect to know right from wrong so that, with spiritual guidance from my church, I could make my own decisions on matters of faith, morals, and integrity. Upon observing the world that I live in, I think that I am well guided in living my life without injuring any one else in any way. I am trying to be as helpful to my fellow man as my condition allows, all in the name and praise of my teacher, my God.

I expect that people would much prefer to read of how I would ask God for guidance and there would be booming voices along with thunder and lightning from Heaven that would provide the answers that I sought. I never experienced this type of interaction. I only have experienced God's guidance and help in more subtle, intellectual ways. Yet, my belief in God is as strong as those who have been witness to a miracle. One of my favorite sayings from the scriptures is from St. Francis, "Preach the gospel at all times, if necessary use words." I try to live my life accordingly.

In my reality, one thinks that one is not judged for his religious fervor, or for his public demonstration of his religious preferences. Rather, one is expressing his religion or acceptance of God through his actions toward his fellow creations every day of his life. I look to all of God's elegant creations when I say this; amoebas, trees, people, and grass. In my world, these creations verify for me that God is. In my world, my world of autism, I find pleasure in just knowing that there is a power that is greater than man. I rejoice with the knowledge that each of God's creations has meaning and value in the "grand plan."

I remember being in church and hearing the priest repeat what Jesus said, "Amen, amen, I say to you, unless you eat the flesh of the son of man and drink his blood, you do not have life within you. Whoever eats my flesh and drinks my blood has eternal life, and I will raise him on the last day. For my flesh is true food, and my blood is true drink. Whoever eats my flesh and drinks my blood remains in me, and I in him. Just as the living Father sent me and I have life because of the Father, so also the one who feeds on me will have life because of me. This is the bread that came down from heaven. Unlike your ancestors who ate and still died, whoever eats this bread will live forever." Unless I remind my self of these words often, I become too involved in the everyday problems of the world and of my life, rapidly forgetting that our savior, Jesus Christ, died for our sins. It is not without regret that I, in my way, understand the relevance of this statement in my belief system.

Question 5: Do you have insights into human civilization? If so, in what ways?

Wally: Without being presumptuous, I will answer this question on the basis of referring to our modern civilization, relying on my observations and insights to guide me. The world that I know, for the most part, is a civilized world according to the definition of civilized; having a highly developed society and culture. Yet, I know that modern man is estranged from this definition in many areas of the world.

Questions have arisen in my mind about how we define the term human civilization as I have listened to the world news of late and reflect on the worldwide human condition based on the news from many different sources and perspectives. I take in every major news report that I can each day. Then, I establish the common thread that is found in the reports on one topic. I discount the reporter's or news service's biases and form my conclusions on the facts that I have gleaned each day from the many reports I have heard. The factual information that I have gleaned does not paint a very optimistic picture that would lead one to believe that our present day human civilization has advanced much, if at all, since our predecessor's time of years ago. From my observations of worldwide news each day, I am too fearful that we humans will ruin our chances of developing one great human civilization if we continue to follow the preexisting course of events that we have been following throughout recorded history. Observe the march of the lemmings and learn from their willingness to follow, without question, their leaders into oblivion.

Reading the daily newspapers, listening to the news on the radio, or watching the evening news as I try to do each day tells me of the uncivilized areas and activities that can be found throughout the world. The people I'm thinking of live in the civilization the world dubs as "modern." Yes, those people who think of themselves as the citizens of the civilized world and members of the human civilization of the 20th and 21st centuries would think again if they took the time and effort to examine their actions and motives.

The question of "Why?" resonates with me each time I hear of the atrocities in the world. The only thing that I can easily understand regarding these excesses of human on human violence is that the perpetrators are terribly failing the civilized world because they too often reflect their own upbringing. The wrinkle in the fabric of human evolution this author recognizes as the Achilles heel in human makeup is that of greed. This is not contained to only thoughts of money and wealth, but encompasses the human appetite for power, and includes the drive to dominate as well. Thankfully, I am not one who is motivated by greed. My motivation only is that of peace and love. This motivates me to want to remember one of my favorite sayings. St Francis once said, "Preach the gospel at all times, if not, use words." I think that the more advanced of our civilizations of today could adopt the spirit of this simple statement when dealing with their own domestic problems and then, this thinking might spread to other cultures worldwide. I realize that this is very simplistic in approaching the problems that face the world today. However, Rome wasn't built in a day, and neither will be the human civilization that I know is possible if we put forth an effective example.

This phenomenon of generational recurring violence, that I eluded to in the previous paragraph, is reaching each quarter of our world and affects each of us in some way. Some of us are being affected directly as with the people of Somalia and the people of the Gaza strip. Then there are those of us in the United States and Great Britain, for example, who are affected indirectly by the wars in other parts of the world. Our jobs, our families, or friends experience what is happening on these fronts, for the most part, indirectly, unless yours is a military family. The only thing that is not affected by this far reaching remote violence in these far off lands is the global weather, and I know that there are some who will claim differently.

My thinking easily revolves around the violence in these areas that I just mentioned as well as places like Iraq, Pakistan, Afghanistan, Chechnya, and some of the political hotspots in Central and South America. Wasting the present youth by either death or by the poisoning of their minds with the venomous rhetoric of an older trusted generation is the usual high priced outcome of such activities. Our civilized world reverberates with the ring of horror at hearing of such senseless excesses that taught hate spawns.

Youthful naiveté along with a poisoned mind and a fanatical penchant for excitement and intrigue fuel the fires of hate in any youthful group of people. Hitler's youth group is one example. Once the seeds of hate are sown in one generation, they reproduce with vigor at an astounding rate which soon accelerates the entire process to a point in some cultures where youth are willing to commit suicide in the name of their cause as in Iraq. The violence cycle repeats itself, raising in our minds the question of why our world's civilization allows this excessive and gruesome activity to occur. Are we not all civilized people on this planet Earth in ways of refraining from man's inhumanity to his fellow man?

I'm particularly realistic in my outlook on world peace, targeting instead world education. The more educated a person is, the less likely he is to be influenced by radical elements in his community. The educated person is more likely to want to think for himself and not be intimidated by the hierarchy that tries to manipulate the masses through group think and mass hysteria as happened in Nazi Germany resulting in World War II and is happening in too many African countries today resulting in the deaths of thousand of innocent people. As reasonable people prevail by reason, those who live by the sword will ultimately die by the sword as evidenced by the demise of ruthless potentates such as Saddam Hussein and his underlings, and the former tyrant of Romania, Ceausescu, and Hitler. Reason rules.

The future of our world civilization will be in the hands of those of us who are educated. By this I certainly don't mean that only people with college degrees are to be considered solely as those who can lead and govern. I mean education in a broader sense that includes being self taught in any number of disciplines which might include electricians, authors, or anyone who is a rational thinker and has common sense. Preventing a person from contributing to the world community that we are all a part of on the basis of his not having a degree or two to wave at people is, in my mind, wrong. Just because a person has one or more degrees does not mean that he is an intelligent person, only that he passed the tests.

To educate the adult population will not be as effective in reducing world violence as would be the education of the youth of the world. Once a person's mind has been exposed to and dulled by violence, with few exceptions, will the person realize the true meaning of world peace. In understanding the mind of a violent person, one has to only look at the actions of

Saddam Hussein's two sons toward the Iraqi people to realize the effects of exposure to violence on a young mind. Other examples of this poisoning of young minds by adults can be found in our culture in the gang violence that is found across our country. One only has to look at our own culture to find many examples where parents are negative role models for their children. This exemplifies the old adage which states violence begets violence.

Human civilization will dominate the world for generations to come. Unless, of course, there is a catastrophic event of some type, i.e., the collision of a meteor, the spread of some uncontrollable pathogen, such as the recent outbreak of swine flu, that would decimate the human population, or the annihilation of man through his own reckless use of nuclear weapons. These occurrences will change the natural course of human evolution and could possibly end human civilization as we know it.

Question 6: Do you have insights into the future of our civilization? If so, in what ways?

Wally: To think that our world is ready to take on the social and economic rigors that would manifest with the creation of one civilization takes much liberty with the perils that history has taught contemporary society. When we look at the great civilizations from our past such as the Roman Empire, the Ottoman Empire, and more recently the British Empire, we can realize that civilizations that have been built from unequal social, and economic groups rarely last for very long before internal struggles, both political and economic, between the constituent groups that make up the artificial union will impede its expansion and its life. The additional added expenses involved in the empire's military activities will slowly drain the coffers of those civilizations that are taxed to support the military activities. When this level of burden is realized by the populous, upheaval and unrest remain the method of resolution.

Eventually, I am convinced the human civilization as we know it will cease to exist. Our civilization will retreat to the point where the world will no longer resemble our 21st century world that we know today. The people of the world will establish once again the separate cultures that were so distinct at the beginning of the 20th century. The pressure to combine all cultures under one world order will not produce a long-term cohesive global community as some people dream of. Reality will prevail when the global community witnesses the inequities that such social restructuring will bring to bare on every socioeconomic group encompassed in such a grandiose plan.

My thoughts are of the recent G-20 summit meeting. The G-20 countries' envoys each returned to their own countries with enough idealism that will not allow them to totally embrace melding with others that attended the summit. There was little agreement between the attendees on most issues that were presented for discussion. In other words, these top economic powers were unable to agree on the most fundamental of questions plaguing each of their economies. With the inability to resolve the economic problems in global fashion, each participant returned to his own country to continue on with their own independent economic practices. Is this the way to work toward one world civilization? Yet, understanding of the other countries' problems is a small step toward the unification of the independent civilizations of the world. We will remain as separate pieces to the puzzle as we now are until we experience global unity through equality on many fronts.

I think that before this experimental artificial exercise can have a ghost of a chance at succeeding, there must be within each group of people, starting with the basic beginnings of the family unit, an equality established worldwide for each member of the family unit. Women must be valued as much as the men. Children of both sexes must be considered as valuable as are their parents. The elderly, frail, and handicapped must be given equal value when compared to the normal population within a given group of people. I will say with certainty that I know of no group that I have experienced to date that fulfills these modest requirements. Until there is equality amongst all human beings on this basic level, worldwide, there is no chance for the long-term unification of all of the ethnic groups who inhabit the world today into one cohesive world civilization. I believe that the civilizations of the world will exist as we now know them, independent of one another, with a modicum of economic, social, and military interaction.

To reiterate, I think that the world civilization that we have been gravitating toward will regroup according to pre-20th century ethnic divisions. The way I point out what I have said is to give you the examples that I have been watching over the years. Look at the retrenching currently taking place in Russia in the past two years. The same can be said for North Korea, as well as Iran. I feel that once the Western presence is diminished in Iraq, the same retrenching will also take place there. When the oil wealth evaporates in the Middle East, what will become of these world powers of today, will they fade into history and become what they once were? Will other oil or energy rich countries be as interested in these oil depleted countries in the future? Realistically, or not, these energy depleted countries will become, in the future, the AIGs of the world as they look for bailouts and economic support so that their hierarchies can continue to enjoy the fruits of others' labor.

Years ago, the world was a place where people were proud of their individual cultures. In the last century this eth- nic enthusiasm was lost because of military and economic factors. Though we are all brothers, we too need to be indi- viduals, equal to each other in political, economic, and social status, and be at peace within our own ethnic groups as well as with all of the other groups throughout the world. When this happens, then maybe the communities of the world could unite into one truly great world civilization. Thoughts of our world at peace find their way into my consciousness, but I know that this is only a dream. To quiet the desire of one culture or group to dominate another culture or group there must be either a need to do so or there must be recognized equality between all factions. I can't say that I have completely experienced this in my country, let alone anything that approaches this recognition of equality on a worldwide level. When this happens, I want history to say that our world has only begun to find the peace that we all pray for in our hearts and minds.

Question 7: Are you fearful or optimistic about your insights?

Wally: Thoughts of the countries of the world retrenching to reestablish their cultural identities is not troubling to me to think about. I think the world is not ready at this point in time to assume one cultural identity. We were trying this concept within our own country, a country of immigrants, a country of blended socioeconomic demographics. Our success in bringing together diverse cultures and looking on them as being equal leaves much to be desired even at this stage in our cultural development. There exists, even now, prejudices amongst the people in our own society. These prejudices are as strong within the same ethnic groups as they are when ethnic groups are pitted against one another as witnessed today in the violence that exists between the Mexicans and the African-Americans in the southwestern USA for example, and in race based gang violence in California. There exists the intra-societal discrimination that is prevalent in more ways than we like to admit. This discrimination is mostly based on difference from the norm. A person is singled out to be ridiculed if he is too tall or too short; too thin or too heavy; too quiet or too boisterous; or too slow or too bright. This discrimination is as scarring as are racial slurs that are done on an inter-racial basis. This type of intra-cultural discrimination is only one of a myriad of issues that stand in the way of all peoples of the world uniting under the umbrella of one great human civilization.

We identify the individual groups that go to make up our society with names such as the African-Americans, the Hispanics, the Native Americans, the Russians, the Irish, etc. After reaching the United States, these groups remain in their own respective communities for a time then they migrate out to reestablish themselves within the broader context of our American society, many times bringing with them their learned prejudices. At times the blending of these groups into the general population of our country is not without prejudice. I point out, for example, the condition of the African-Americans, Hispanics, Native Americans, Asians, and Middle Easterners in our society even when these people are industrious, and have made significant progress themselves in trying to become assimilated into the American way of life. Their physical and cultural differences make them targets of inequality in our society. Yet, each individual is equal in the eyes of God.

The people mentioned above, plus others, are ostracized from the American dream because they remain enough different from those who have inherited their rights by virtue of being in this country for many generations. In this light, I find it difficult to believe that, worldwide, this notion of one unified civilization will work at this point in human history. I think in time, the individual civilizations of the world will become involved with each other to the extent that there will be more economic and social equality than there is at present. When this happens, the miscibility of multiple civilizations into one great civilization will become more of a reality. I am optimistic that in time, our human capacity to think will replace our ability to wage war, and then, the human civilization that is dreamt of will become a reality. Time is only the willing ally of such an endeavor.

Popular support for uniting the civilizations of the world is not, in my opinion, at a point where there could be viability in such notions. Yet, our global interests seem to indicate something different. We and other world powers, "in the interest of humanity," are more than willing to exercise influence on any country where we can gain a foothold. China in Somalia; the United States in Poland and Iraq; North Korea in South Korea; Russia in some of its former satellites like Georgia are examples of this. Yet, the powers of the world are not all the benevolent idealists that they want us to believe they are. Though I think that there is a faction within each country that I just mentioned that seeks peace, understanding, and equality with its global neighbors, the power structure in these countries is focused on dominance, either military or economic. In light of these goals, I don't have much optimism when it comes to the development of an idealistic world civilization. To walk in the footsteps of our predecessors is not the answer to the question of how do we achieve global harmony. The unification of the world's people into one great civilization will take place when all of mankind defers to the highest power that some people refer to as God, all in their own way.

Question 8: Do you believe your insights will manifest or are they only forecasts?

Wally: I want to believe that in my lifetime there will be peace and understanding between all people of the world. However, being the realist that I am, I will not hold my breath until this happens. The people within each country and ethnic group first have to make peace with themselves. This is a necessary step that must be taken before they can look to influence the world at large in matters of peace, equality, and human rights;

all hallmarks of great societies and civilizations throughout history.

I remind you of our own country, Ireland, India, and China, to name a few of the countries where internal problems among their own people would keep them from the one world civilization that is thought of by many. These countries are only a few that I mention to illustrate my point that inequality and the political and socioeconomic barriers still exist within each of these countries. I realize that thinking like I do about the issues that face the civilizations of the world that we live in today will invite much criticism by those who think otherwise. However, I think that my forecasts about the countries of the world retrenching to recoup their own identities is a fact that is worth considering. The omission of the bare facts of any situation when considering their consequences will place us in the realm of the weather forecaster who has the benefit of modern technology at his disposal but is usually right about 50 percent of the time.

Reaching any conclusions about my insights will require the expert voices of the past that will quickly repeat the words of their predecessors to prove their points. The past holds the keys to the future of human civilization and it must be remembered that these keys from the past are not always in concert with our own contemporary ideas. With our thoughts and ideas we think that man can accomplish the impossible. However, these thoughts and ideas must first be implemented before there is progress that our civilization will continue to advance. We are estranged from our roots by the equation that quantifies human progress as being equal to a total of power over people plus material wealth. The thoughts about unifying the peoples of the world will take hold once the equation factors in variables such as love, understanding, respecting human life, and respecting the creations of nature. Thinking quietly, I repeat over and over to my self the questions that we humans face today and find that most can be answered in a spiritually satisfying way only if we refer to the Ten Commandments that were given to us by God.

Question 9: What can we do to guide and inform others (including non-believers) about such insights?

Wally: We should perhaps print up some type of historical perspective that would illustrate in clear precise language the history of human civilization from as far back in history as there is reliable information. This could show in brief scenarios the milestones that are considered to be significant in the progress or lack thereof in the development of our human civilization. This compilation of information could be the basis for a course taught in schools and universities. It could be known as "The History of Human Civilization." I wonder why no one has thought of this previously, or have they?

In our minds, the idea of our present civilization as being the epitome of humanism registers some questions in the minds of those of us who have the time and inclination to think in depth about such questions. We would question the idea that contemporary societies worldwide are ahead of our predecessors, both early and of late, in the actual placement of our civilization on as high a plain as we currently are lead to believe. For sure, there are more consumer goods, more tools to make our lives easier than they were several hundred years ago. These pretences add a certain amount of luxury to our lives. However, when looking to their standing in improving human civilization, the apparent benefits in some cases are cancelled out by the unseen or hidden realities of their production.

For example, the computer revolution of the past 30 or 40 years has enhanced the lives of many people worldwide thus creating the illusion that this one technology will raise our civilization worldwide to new levels. This might for some societies, like ours, be true. However, if one considers the global effects of the computer revolution the picture of its successes in making life better for some is in part obscured for others when the total effects of worldwide computerization is taken into account.

The real progress in worldwide civilization is somewhat diminished when the total effects on our ecology and human health are factored in. Is our world civilization better off or farther ahead than it would be if there were no computers? When one considers the effects of producing the computers on our total world, the picture changes. Though I am only a nonverbal autistic person, I recognize that the production of computers worldwide has a negative as well as a positive influence on our planet. The plastic components of the computers are derived from petroleum products, which themselves have real environmental impacts, usually negative when one considers their extraction, their refining, the end products of their use and distribution in the form of greenhouse gasses and other pollution.

The plastics represent only a part of the problem. The same type of scenario can be projected for each type of computer component. The energy requirements to produce, distribute, and operate the computers must also be factored into the total equation as well as the effects on the environment of this energy consumption.

This look at the computer's production costs in terms of global effects is only a part of the picture. In addition, one has to look at the effects of the outdated electronic equipment on the world ecology and on the health of not only the workers in countries like China who scavenge the outdated equipment for recycling purposes, but for the thousands of people living downwind or down stream of the recycling operations. These people, not directly involved in the manufacture, use, or recycling of outdated electronic equipment, are negatively affected. Nations that recycle the spent electronics will waste their youth in such endeavors. Will subsequent generations also be affected by the aftermath of this pollution? Perhaps.

Will our civilization have a net advancement from the use of electronics including computers? Perhaps, but not as much as it might first appear.

I think that each era in human civilization reaches a pinnacle, then slides back to some previous level, then is overtaken by some other civilization that is on the upswing. Our own civilization is subject to this same type of development, decline, and obliteration that I mentioned above. This cycling of civilizations warns us of our vulnerability. If we look to those previous civilizations that were at one time the greatest civilizations in the world i.e., the Greeks, Romans, Mesopotamians, Incas, Mayans, and Egyptians, to name a few, we can learn from their histories and put what we have learned from them into our modern context so that we might be able to stop history from repeating itself.

Recent developments worldwide will essentially prove my arguments as I presented in my previous answers. Europeans, even the Queen of England, want to retrench or assume their political, economic, and social identities as of this recent G-20 conference. In my realizing this, Obama was not as effective in his attempts to unify the world as he expected he would have been given the popular support he was used to during his European visit while campaigning for the presidency. Will the leaders of Europe and the rest of the world see the United States now as Germany has? I think that we people in the United States have witnessed our place on the worldwide stage usurped by old rivals that were, as recently as two or three decades ago, economic, social, and political drains on the rest of the world. Take China, India, and the European Union countries as examples of this. I expect this slide of our power and world standing to continue down hill for the foreseeable future. Reality will return to the world in a few years as will our leadership role once "we get our own house in order."

Question 10: What would you wish for the average reader to understand about what you've shared?

Wally: The people who read my answers to the questions that Bill asked will each no doubt take something different from them. This is how it should be. Each reader has a different background and therefore will approach each question from his own perspective and take from the answers that which has some relevance for him. I would like to think that I might have, in some small way, answered for the reader a question or two that they may have had. If I have achieved this, then I will be happy. If I have upset anyone I am truly sorry because I didn't expect that my answers would foster any negative reactions. If I have enlightened or gave cause to think to even one person, I will consider my efforts to be well rewarded.

For me, if the reader will understand that the thoughts and ideas that they have read were those of a nonverbal autistic person, I will have achieved complete satisfaction and will say that I have bridged the gap that exists between "their world" and "my world" of the nonverbal autistic. To bring your thinking to other people so that they can understand you is the pinnacle of the linking of minds so that one person can express his thoughts to others and be understood by them. This connecting of minds is the beginning of human civilization that is the extension and personification of the human soul.

The question of the world civilization will reverberate through the minds and hearts of many for years to come. These ideas have, no doubt, been with people since there was recognizable human thought. However, the reality of one cohesive human civilization inhabiting the world is too fanciful to be practical at this point. I believe that the world will be populated by many separate civilizations, each with its distinctions, and each at a different stage of social, economic, and political evolution. With these diverse cultures and civilizations come the inherent problems of economic, social, and political inequality on many fronts. It will be millennia before these problems are resolved.

Years ago, I thought that I was an ether spirit in Wally's body, now I know that I am a being with a body, mind, intellect and soul. I now know that we will truly thank the spirits of our ancestors when we look to their wisdom and insight into our current problems. They saw us not as thoughts in the future but as reflections of themselves in the universe that was too complex for them to understand.

Oceans of the universe reach our world's shores as the quasars become dim with time. Years will pass with waves of universal halos reaching each mind as if our ancestors wanted to keep the world bathed in the thoughts of past civilizations so that we might learn from them, not because they had found all of the answers, but because they realized that they had made mistakes.

The thoughts that we want to share with our unborn generations years in the future are only in our minds until we recite them to another, and to another, and to another.... In this way we teach these future generations that we were. To pass information on to other people and to other generations is perhaps why we are here. If the ideas escape the words of a generation, then they are lost to the distant stars. Would you please teach me to express myself to others so that my ideas will always be on the minds of those who come after me? I teach those who will listen to me that in their minds ideas will not bring them fame or peace. Ideas will only make them think more of their past. This is the point I want to make. The past and the future are now in our minds. The End.

Chapter 9

Conclusions

*"So I gain truth when I expand my constricted eye, an eye
that has only let in what I have been taught to see."*
—Minnie Bruce Pratt

As I began to analyze the outcomes of the questionnaire, I realized there remained one more person who had yet to take it: me. I was so busy gathering information and cross-referencing it that I had overlooked the fact that I, too, should be counted among those who have something to contribute by answering the survey.

Question 1: What are your earliest memories of being in the world?

My earliest recollection is nothing otherworldly or terribly impressive: I was an infant having his diaper changed by my babysitting, teenage aunt when I suddenly let loose a stream of urine that made an arc through the air, wetting her in the process. I probably retain this memory because of the reactive yelp my poor aunt gave, in addition to the sensation that I had done something wrong.

That aside, I have other early recollections, not of people but of *things*—my parents' black Morris Minor; sunglasses with green lenses; Leslie, my blonde troll doll; the concrete birdbath in my grandparents' backyard; the visual distortions created by peering through the multifaceted crystal knife rest on the dining room table; how the funeral home's nighttime neon sign would light only so much as to read, "FUN HOME"; or the publisher's colophon of a striding man at the base of a book spine that I associated in memory with FTD's similar logo of the winged messenger—odd, fragmented bits and pieces that you might expect of someone who is attentive to the details that are often unobserved by others.

Question 2: Have you always had an understanding of your place in the world?

Yes, I always had a sense of having known wealth and privilege, and, even as a young child, I would pose for pictures with a precocious, aristocratic air. I've never been at a loss for anything material only things *emotional*. (I generally disdain celebrity and finances and have no interest in either, perhaps because of this feeling of prior entitlement.) In my darkest hour, in which I seriously contemplated suicide as an adolescent, what prevented me from taking my life was a clarion understanding that I was destined to become known for what I could offer others. At the time, I had no clue what that meant or what it would look like; it is clear to me now.

Question 3: Have you sensed a divine presence (such as God) close to you? If so, has it been consistent throughout your life?

I have always felt a very strong protective presence around me, insulating me and saving me in the eleventh hour. This has strengthened as I've aged, but it goes beyond luck or good fortune. I have never been seriously ill, I've never been hospitalized, I've never been in a serious accident of any kind, I've never had a broken bone, nor have I ever been in a situation in which I thought my life was endangered. Even in the times I was physically bullied and assaulted at school, I was more shaken and rattled than harmed. In fact, everything I could've possibly wanted in life—from material possessions to experiential opportunities—has all come my way. I recognize that this is highly unusual and, believe me, I don't take it for granted. Not for a moment. I believe such privilege comes with great responsibility, and I endeavor to use my extraordinary good fortune in ways that might benefit others.

Question 4: Does this divine presence guide and inform you? If so, in what ways?

I believe we are all guided throughout each day by a divine presence in the guise of our conscience. Because we are blessed with free will, we can elect to ignore it, but still it remains, encouraging us to do the right thing. I think we are also mentored and guided in dreams, although the symbolisms may more readily be interpreted by our souls than by our conscious selves. I am aware of a guiding presence that impresses ingenuity and inspiration within me every day, and I express gratitude for that.

Question 5: Do you have insights into human civilization? If so, in what ways?

Because I am not a social person, I oftentimes feel more like an anthropologist, carefully observing, always filtering my encounters with others through the universal sieve of the grand scheme: What did he just learn from that? Does she realize how her words just impacted others? Does he understand how this relates to something else? I always see myself from the solar system looking down objectively on humankind, connecting the dots to appreciate why things happen the way they do. As much as I attempt to recognize altruism, and acknowledge it wherever possible, I also see the great indifference and disregard people hold for one another.

Question 6: Do you have insights into the future of our civilization? If so, in what ways?

I don't in particular, but I do sense people slowly dividing into two camps: those who are selfish and self-absorbed, manipulative and duplicitous, and those who "get it" by routinely practicing selflessness toward others. Perhaps this alludes to the spiritual warfare examined in Chapter 5; that is, a pervasive, ill-intended presence forcing us into the division I am observing.

Question 7: Are you fearful or optimistic about your insights?

Ambivalent, I suspect. I wish only to do my part by contributing to the efforts of the latter camp in the hopes of swaying those in the former camp.

Question 8: Do you believe your insights will manifest or are they only forecasts?

I do believe that, before long, we will draw closer and closer to a time when misbehavior and inconsiderate conduct will not be tolerated. I believe there will come a time to reclaim grace and dignity but not without great loss. This is not necessarily a bad thing, it is a learning opportunity.

Question 9: What can we do to guide and inform others (including non-believers) about such insights?

Know yourself honestly and fully, and focus upon doing that which is right and true and good and kind. There is much hate to dismantle—all of it ego driven.

Question 10: What would you wish for the average reader to understand about what you've shared?

That we are all truly brothers of one another and every one of us *matters*.

A SPIRITUAL INFLUENCE

As I suspected, I heard from many parents of children with autism who offered to complete the survey on behalf of their children, but this I expressly disallowed. The intent of the survey was for persons on the autism spectrum, themselves, to respond. In those cases, the individuals (for whom caregivers were enquiring) were unable to speak, which left me to wonder if their intellect was being presumed and if they had an alternative mode of communication in lieu of spoken language.

Two themes seem most consistent in the responses: a sense of faith in God, and a great concern for the future of our planet. With regard to the former, I was pleased to read Michael's affirming validation, "God does not leave the defenseless alone." I have long believed that people with autism know, for the most part, what they're in for when they are born into this world; and I have also felt that when one selects such a challenging life, one is not thrust into it to fend for one's self without spiritual guidance, support, and mentoring. In addressing the latter concern for the welfare of Earth, there are admissions that we are, indeed, in trouble but the majority of replies project that this is correctible if we unite to honor our environment with respect.

Some of those polled may sound somewhat misanthropic—I understand and appreciate their position, and how the world can wear you down such that depression colors your perceptions. I, too, was spiritually blocked and embittered for many years of my own life, inhibited from being as compassionate as I now am.

Perhaps the most profound perspectives came from those that I know are individuals living in silence—yet communicate using speech alternatives—and who experience absorbing periods of solitude: Karly, Michael, and Izzy among them. Others, like Nick, have come to a place of understanding previously unattained earlier in life, "The world is shrinking and with each succeeding generation, we are beginning to realize that we are all a part of each other. We rise or fall...sink or swim together. Our very survival depends on this realization."

Another prominent theme was the desire to simply be believed and valued as equal contributors; and this speaks to the manner in which people, who have clinical diagnoses that suggest intellectual inferiority, may often be maligned or patronized (more so than the average person) for what they communicate—if they are even able to do so. As Mark observes, "Be sure to accept us as real people and respect our talents. It is hard to do because we can look different and sometimes act weird. But give us a chance to prove our worth."

Surprisingly so, for a people subjugated, there are no threats of retaliation and no eternal damnation predicted; and precious little in terms of fatalistic hellfire and brimstone. Nor is there a day of reckoning foreseen by which poetic justice is granted through punitive retribution of those who have mocked and degraded those disabled. On the contrary, despite sometimes inhumane tribulations, a sense of graceful perseverance pervades the responders' replies. For the most part, there is optimism for our future as a human race. There is faith. And there is hope.

END OF DAYS?

Prophets, psychics, seers, and frauds have predicted the end of days since prehistoric times. Such doomsday predictions may come as a scare-tactic warning that our race should shape up and change its evil ways, or it may be a way to exert some measure of control over the unknown—our future. Most recently there has been lots of buzz about the impending year 2012, the end of the Mayan calendar, and what relevance that holds for us. As a young child, I was often overwhelmed with anxiety about future events over which I had little control *because of* my desire to exercise control. From my childhood home I could glimpse—on a hillside in the distance—the high school I would be attending a decade in the future; and still I agonized worrying over the logistics of catching the bus to get there when the time came! (Next, I lost sleep over the scheduled transition to the metric system which, mercifully, never transpired.)

A few years later I read a book, *Beyond the Strange*, about unusual phenomenon (which I still have and which I dug up to re-examine) that claimed, "These stories…are truly unbelievable—and, unbelievably, *true*." In it there were a couple of sections about people who were reputedly gifted visionaries for predicting future events. One of them, Edgar Cayce, an enigmatic seer with a large following, was credited with forecasting that the eastern United States, including New York City, would be destroyed in the 1990s. Another entry told of Mother Shipton, an English soothsayer who lived in the 1500s and told fortunes that reportedly foreshadowed modern events with accuracy. The book quotes Mother Shipton's most famous prediction, "The world then to an end will come in nineteen hundred and ninety-one."

Obviously the 1990s have come and gone without these major catastrophes coming to fruition. (I have since learned that Mother Shipton's original quote, in fact, referenced 1881—*not* 1991!) But can you imagine being a young boy with Asperger's Syndrome who interprets most everything literally and is so impressionable as to *believe* what he was reading in 1972 because it was touted as "unbelievably true"? And believe me, I worried about 1991 for nearly 20 years after the fact. (Anyone interested in understanding the extent of anxiety in persons like myself should avail themselves of Nick Dubin's excellent book, *Asperger and Anxiety*.) My point is that I now bristle at the arrogance of any human being who presumes the authority to have all the answers; if we did, we wouldn't be human. And we would never appreciate the beauty of the mysterious.

This is not to suggest that we should be dismissive of the informative viewpoints illuminated in this volume. There is great value for appreciating the insights of detail-oriented and observant citizens who are often highly-intuitive and very sensitive. In his book, *Putting on the Mind of Christ* (Hampton Roads Publishing Company, 2000), Jim Marion, a contemporary mystic and former Catholic monk, asserts, "As long as modern-day Christianity does not accept prophetic messages from modern-day prophets, they are missing out on a great deal of wise information coming through to us today." Bearing this truth are St. Paul's letters to the Corinthians, found in the New Testament, which not only speak of the potential for such gifts (devoid of any evil connotations) but reinforce their accessibility to us all.

As much as others are engrossed with combating autism, its increasing and inexplicable prevalence commands a respite for recognition— a moment of cease-fire from the battle to reassess and re-evaluate its meaning. To this end, recall the simplicity of young Fred's candid explanation, "Autism is telling my world that it is not paying attention to the signs." In reviewing the collective (and remarkably consistent) responses to my spirituality poll from our gentle comrades, one may make the reasonable argument that we, in fact, most definitely *need* more people like them in the world—people who are considerate, passionate, intuitive, and who see the big picture with lucidity.

Humankind is not without mission, and people with autism contribute purpose to that end: evolving, improving, creating, and collaborating for the mutual betterment of one another. Despite—or because of—being marginalized as disabled, those deigned less than perfect are challenged to occupy the same space as "normals" with the entitlement of human equanimity—therein lies the struggle. Remember: resistance of acceptance is not a fear of our differences but a fear of confronting our *similarities*. To wit, a mother from Belgium once wrote me, "My son [with autism] told me one time, 'I came on the earth to bring peace, but it's more difficult than I could imagine.'"

Please don't misinterpret this book by sensationalizing its content in the extreme, or by stigmatizing those with autism unreasonably as "God's special little angels." I have never deliberately glorified anyone with autism in such a manner though certain others have chosen to perceive it otherwise. I do, though, believe we are nearing a renaissance of truth and enlightenment—a time of grace and healing and unity—and everyone should be afforded the opportunity to participate by employing their spiritual gifts and talents to the fullest—the ability to do so lies within us *all*. It's not beyond our means, it is *within* our means. And it is driven, artfully, by love and compassion and a desire to be of service to others.

Because we are all at different points on life's learning curve, this will be a process. Some of us, such as many on the autism spectrum, are naturally more introspective and better attuned with our higher selves than others. Educational tiers make an apt analogy: those at university must bring along others still in grammar school, and we'll all need to be especially diligent to motivate those held back to repeat a grade—or two. Our race has historically been granted infinite opportunities to get it right, to overcome dire consequences, and to learn from our transgressions. Failure is not an option; but is an end of days imminent if we falter? No, I think not. God will remain patient with us as we evolve the human journey. But, then again, I'm inspired to pause in reflection of my friend Izzy's wise and humble words, "Only God knows exactly what the future will hold.

Index

abortion, 165

accounts, amazing, 68-72

Act, Americans with Disabilities, 15

Administration, Health Resources and Services, 18

angels, 114

Animals in Translation, 24

antidote, love as an, 118-120

Arendt, Hannah, 12

art of healing, the, 29

Asperger and Anxiety, 199

auditory stimuli, 77-78

Autism and the God Connection, 11, 19, 23, 38, 57

Autism Research Centre, 13

Autism, The Soul of, 11, 13, 19, 25, 35, 38, 65

autism treatments, 52

Baron-Cohen, Professor Simon, 13

Beacon That Beckons, The, 19-20

Beyond the Strange, 198-199

bilocation, 71-72

birth, remembering, 139, 164-165

bleed-over, 136

Capra, Fritjof, 73

Carrie, 64

Chad, Championing, 26

Children of the New Millennium, 130

clairalience, 135

clairambiance, 135

clairaudience, 135

clairgustance, 135

clairsentience, 135

clairvoyance, 135

code, our moral, 19

Congressional Budget Committee, 27

consciousness, the dichotomy of, 53

curiouser and curiouser, 63-68

days, end of, 198-200

demon recruitment, 113

demons, ghost or, 88

devil in the details, 92-96

dichotomy of consciousness, 53

divine presence, sensing a, 141-146, 171-177

earliest memories, 138-139

Einstein, Albert, 135, 163

electricity, interference of, 92

end of days, 198-200

energy,
    spheres of, 83-84
    undisciplined, 35-43

environmental improvements, 157

evolution, a rising, 16-19

Exorcist, The, 113, 116

eyes, red, 91

Facilitated Communication, 27 (see also FC)

FC, 56-60, 131, 140, 141

Francis, St., 176, 179

frontiers, final, 72-76

ghosts or demons, 88

Gifts of the Spirit, 136

Gifts, Impossible, 51-76

God, being with, 139

Grandin, Temple, 24

guidance from a divine presence, 141-146, 171-177

healers, natural born, 32-33

healing in practice, 41-43

healing,
    a predisposition for, 43-48
    my gift of, 40-41
    the Art of, 29-48

Health and Human Services, U.S. Department of, 18-19

human civilization, insights into, 147-149, 177-184, 195

humiliation, mistreatment and, 12

ill intent, discerning, 91-92

illusion, life is an, 158

immune system, depleting the, 37

in utero, recollections of stimuli, 165

influence, spiritual, 197-198

insights, manifesting, 153-156, 186-187, 196

insights,
    feeling about personal, 151-153, 184-186, 195-196
    informing others about, 154-156, 188-191, 196

Intense World Syndrome, 44-46

intent, discerning ill, 91-93

interaction or conversation with an unseen presence, a two-way, 81

Jewishfuture.com, 128, 130, 131, 132

knowledge is power, 77-85

levitation, 75

Lifetimes, being aware of other, 141

love as an antidote, 118

love, king of, 27-28

Magic 8-Ball, 137

manifestation of insights, 153-154, 186-187

mantra versus stimming, 34

Masters, The Dancing Wu Li, 74

Mayan calendar, 198

Mechanics of Miracles, the, 23-28

mind games, 56-63

mind, the healing of the, 24

Miracles, A Course in, 24

Miracles, the Mechanics of, 23-28

mistreatment and humiliation, 12

mix, an eclectic, 64-68

moral code, our, 19

Musicophilia, 34

National Survey of Children's Health, 18

Nazareth, Jesus of, 72

net, casting the, 135-162

Neuroscience, Frontiers in, 44

night terrors, 91

Nun, The Flying, 75

Obsessive Compulsive Disorder (OCD), see 58

Origins of Totalitarianism, The, 12

pain or discomfort, undetected, 90

Paracelsus, Philipus Aureolus, 29

Past, Our Egregious, 14-15

Pennhurst State School, 15

pets, clingy, 92

phantom, year of the, 96-113

Physics, The Tao of, 73

power struggle, 116-118

power, knowledge is, 77-85

practice, healing in, 41-43

Pratt, Minnie Bruce, 193

prayer savings account, 174

Project, Vaccine Autoimmune, 16

protocol, spiritual, 79-83

Putting on the Mind of Christ, 199

questionnaire, crafting a, 132-134

recruitment, demon, 113

red eyes, 91

Reiki, 29-31, 66-67

remedy for healing with one's own energy, 38-39

Results and responses to the questionnaire, 135-162

retaliation, 120-123

revelation, a remarkable, 127-133

Revelation, the Book of, 117

Risperdal, 91, 105, 106

savings account, prayer, 174

shamans, healing as the Mexican, 42

Shipton, Mother, 198

sleep issues, 91

smells and tastes, 78

Soul of Autism, The, 11, 13, 19, 25, 35, 38, 65

Spheres of Energy, 83-84

Spirit, Gifts of the, 136

spiritual influence, 197-198

spiritual stimuli, 79-83

spiritual warfare, 87-124

St. Francis, 176, 179

Star Trek, 76

"stimming," the value of, 33-35

stimuli, assaultive environmental, 77-78

Strange, Beyond the, 198-199

Supper, the Last, 72

Survey, U.S. Religious Landscape, 20

Syndrome, Intense World, 44-46

Tao of Physics, The, 73

terrors, night, 91

touch, 78

Truth, The Ascent to, 118

understanding your place in the world, 140-141, 167-171, 194

Vaccine Autoimmune Project, 16

victims, perfect, 89-90

visual stimuli, 77

Wally's Wisdom, 163-192

Warfare, Spiritual, 87-124

wills, two, 167

Wisdom, Wally's, 163-192

world, understanding your place in the, 140-141, 167-171, 194

About the Author

William Stillman has been dubbed "The Autism Whisperer," by talk-show host Frankie Picasso, for his innate ability to understand and interpret children and adults on the autism spectrum. Lisa Jo Rudy, About.com's autism moderator, has said, "William Stillman is one of the few who can translate the workings of the autistic mind to the neuro-typical community."

He is an award-winning writer, and the author of *Demystifying the Autistic Experience: A Humanistic Introduction for Parents, Caregivers and Educators*, which has been highly praised by the autism and self-advocacy communities. His other books include *Empowered Autism Parenting, The Autism Answer Book, The Everything Parent's Guide to Children with Asperger's Syndrome, When Your Child Has Asperger's Syndrome, The Everything Parent's Guide to Children with Bipolar Disorder, Autism and the God Connection*, and *The Soul of Autism*.

Stillman has written for *The Huffington Post, Basil and Spice, The Autism Perspective, Autism Voices and Choices*, and *Autism-at-Home Series*. The dance company, dre.dance, cited Stillman's autism writings as an inspiration for its 2009 choreography performance, *beyond. words*, which had its New York premiere at Tribeca Performing Arts

Center. (Stillman is also coauthor of several successful books about his life-long passion, *The Wizard of Oz*.)

Autism and the God Connection, Stillman's study of profound spiritual, mystical, and metaphysical giftedness of some individuals with autism, has resonated with parents, professionals, and persons with autism internationally, and has received endorsements of praise from best-selling authors Gary Zukav, Carol Bowman, Dean Hamer, and Larry Dossey. It was a finalist for Publishers Marketing Association's Benjamin Franklin Award for excellence. Stillman's *The Soul of Autism* was an award-winning finalist for *USA Book News*'s National Best Books Awards, and was judged a Silver Award Winner by Nautilus Book Awards. Inspired by *Autism and the God Connection*, Stillman hosted a monthly question-and-answer column for *Children of the New Earth* online magazine, and he has developed an autism guide for The Thoughtful Christian, a theological training and resource organization. The film rights to *Autism and the God Connection* and *The Soul of Autism* have been optioned for a proposed documentary. Both *Autism and the God Connection* and *The Soul of Autism* were translated by German publisher Amra Verlag.

As an adult with Asperger's Syndrome, a mild "cousin" of autism, Stillman's message of reverence and respect has touched thousands nationally through his acclaimed autism workshops and private consultations throughout the United States. Stillman has a B.S. in Education from Millersville University in Pennsylvania, and has worked to support people with different ways of being since 1987. He was formerly the Pennsylvania Department of Public Welfare, Office of Developmental Programs' statewide point person for children with intellectual impairment, mental health issues, and autism.

Stillman is founder of the Pennsylvania Autism Self Advocacy Coalition (PASAC) which endeavors to educate and advise state and local government, law enforcement, educators, and the medical community about the autism spectrum from the "inside out." He served on Pennsylvania's Autism Task Force, and is on several autism advisory boards. He is formerly the coordinator for a Pennsylvania-based meeting group of individuals who use Augmentative and Alternative Communication. Stillman was also instrumental in guiding and directing

Youth Advocate Programs, Inc. relationship-based autism training curriculum. At present, he consults for New Light, Inc.

In his work to support those who love and care for individuals with autism and Asperger's Syndrome, Stillman sets a tone for our collective understanding of the autistic experience in ways that are unprecedented. Autism should not be defined as an "affliction endured by sufferers," but as a truly unique and individual experience to be respected and appreciated by all. In so doing, Stillman highlights the exquisite sensitivities of our most valuable, wise, and loving "teachers."

William Stillman's Website is *www.williamstillman.com.*